THE GOLDEN AGE
OF *Newport Yachting*

BETWEEN THE WARS

ROBERT B. MACKAY

THE
History
PRESS

Published by The History Press
Charleston, SC
www.historypress.com

Front cover, top, left to right: Launches from great motor yachts pick up owners and guests on the landing stage of the New York Yacht Club's station at Newport before the second race for the America's Cup on August 2, 1937. *Author's collection*; H. Edward and Estelle Manville aboard their new million-dollar yacht, *Hi-Esmaro*, with their captain on the right. *Author's collection*; The magnificent 272-foot, turboelectric *Viking* (II). *The Mariners' Museum and Park*; *bottom*: *Squadron at Newport*, by Warren Sheppard (1858–1937). *Author's collection*.
Back cover: *Nourmahal's* (III) library. *The Edwin Levick Collection, Mariners' Museum and Park, 96434. inset*: Howard Hughes and Ginger Rogers. *Author's collection*.

First published 2021

Manufactured in the United States

ISBN 9781467149372

Library of Congress Control Number: 2021931139

Notice: The information in this book is true and complete to the best of our knowledge. It is offered without guarantee on the part of the author or The History Press. The author and The History Press disclaim all liability in connection with the use of this book.

To Julian "Dooley" K. Roosevelt (1924–1986) and Henry "Harry" H. Anderson Jr. (1921–2020), mentors well versed in the lore of yachting.

CONTENTS

CONTENTS

PROLOGUE AND
ACKNOWLEDGEMENTS

Newport can tell many stories well, as evidenced by the wealth of books published over the last few decades on aspects of its history and architectural heritage. The great houses lining Bellevue Avenue are as well known and celebrated as any of their period in the country, and the names of the barons of American commerce who built them are still remembered. Yet the same cannot be said for the resort's floating adjunct, the magnificent yachts that were anchored down in the harbor and the affluent jack-tars who sailed them. Here we explore this lesser-known story, one that was of great consequence to Newport and its development.

Choosing just whom to profile has been a difficult task and is not intended to be comprehensive. Many of the names will be familiar to the reader, but among the nautically inclined, "cottagers" who might have been included are Auchinclosses, Berwinds, Browns, Havemeyers, Osgoods, Stillmans and Strawbridges, to mention just a handful. Nor was there room for all of the affluent habitués of the harbor and Brenton Cove, who never had cottages but made their seasonal presence known aboard their opulent craft. Yachtsmen such as E.F. Hutton, whose 202-foot *Hussar IV* and 316-foot *Hussar V* (later renamed *Sea Cloud* after his divorce from Marjorie Merriweather Post) were hard to miss, or Carl Tucker, transportation magnate Anthony Nicholas Brady's son-in-law and the owner of the huge 223-foot, three-masted schooner *Migrant*. Preference was given to a good story, and in some cases, timing was a factor. John Nicholas Brown raced his old Herreshoff schooner *Saraband* (ex-*Irolita*) in the late 1930s, but his moment in the annals of yachting would come after the war with his legendary ocean racer, *Bolero*, and in the case of the Vanderbilts and their yachts, a saga worthy of volumes, we deal here only with those who were of greatest consequence for Newport between the world wars.

This book has grown out of a talk I gave in 2016 at the Newport Symposium on "Newport's Gilded Age Yachtsmen" and would not have been possible without the advice, assistance and encouragement of many who were intrigued by the topic. My hat is off first to Trudy Coxe, CEO and executive director of the Preservation Society of Newport County, and her 2016 symposium director, Dr. Laurie Ossman.

Long a mentor whose extraordinary participation in the pastime began between the world wars, the late Henry H. "Harry" Anderson generously shared his observations on yachting history, as has Roger Vaughan, author of the excellent new biographies on both Harry and his relative Arthur Curtiss James. Robert Manice and archivist Bill Speck have been my guides to Goelet's remarkable role in the development of yachting. Earl McMillen III, Lisette Prince de Ramel, Diana Prince and family historian Eileen Warburton have shed light on Frederick H. Prince's years afloat. The late Anthony Baker and Clarence Michalis shared their recollections of George F. Baker's *Viking*. Bertram Lippincott III of the Newport Historical Society generously shared his remarkable knowledge of the "City by the Sea." Spencer C. McCombs of Cordtsen Design Architecture kindled my appreciation of Red Cross Cottage while Jesse Brody was my guide to the Drexel University Archives. The New York Yacht Club's curator of collections, Alice Dickinson, and librarian Vanessa Cameron were my pilots to the resources of their institution.

The images between these pages were drawn from my own collection and a wide range of private and public sources. Special thanks are due to MaryAnne Stets, curator of photography; Maureen A.J. Smith, intellectual property coordinator; Carol Mowrey and Krystal Rose at Mystic Seaport Museum for their assistance with the Rosenfeld Collection. Sara Puckitt, curator of photography at the Mariner's Museum and Park, was my guide to their Levick Collection. Other images have been drawn from Historic New England, Newport Historical Society and the New York Yacht Club, the Suffolk Vanderbilt Museum and the Roosevelt-Vanderbilt National Historic Site.

Sandy Branciforte transcribed the manuscript and had many sage suggestions along the way. Harriet G. Clark, with whom I've sailed many miles, generously participated in the wordsmithing and editing while my wife, Anna, exhibited remarkable patience as she lost access to her dining room table for many months to a tsunami of books and papers.

INTRODUCTION

G ardner Dunton, covering the resumption of the America's Cup competition in 1958, the first match since World War II, was dismayed. Newport, he felt, was "making but a feeble attempt" to replicate the "extravagant magnificence" of "the races of former years,"[1] which in the 1930s had taken place at the height of the season and were now scheduled for the end of September—and in twelve-meter sloops, mere dinghies in comparison to the towering and majestic J-boats that had competed before the war. The "glamour of 1937," the "palatial yachts" that had followed the races, were now gone.[2] Arthur Curtiss James's magnificent three-masted barkentine *Aloha*, a symphony in canvas and the flagship of the pastime, had been scrapped even before the war began. George F. Baker's huge turbo-electric *Viking*, H.E. Manville's beautiful *Hi-Esmaro* and Willie K. Vanderbilt's world traveler *Alva* had all been sunk in the naval service during the war, and their owners were dead. J.P. Morgan, Frederick H. Prince and Cornelius Vanderbilt, who had been so visible in '37, had also sailed their last voyages, Morgan's famous *Corsair* (IV) ending its days on a reef off Acapulco, Prince's *Lone Star* still upright but on the bottom off Cape May and Vanderbilt's sleek flyer *Winchester* (IV) rusting away in a Canadian port after its war service there. Vincent Astor's 263-foot flagship *Nourmahal*, from whose decks President Roosevelt had seen the 1934 America's Cup, was still afloat, a forgotten hulk in a government mothball fleet.

The swank New York Yacht Club station, which in 1937 had "hummed with activity," with stewards "calling out the arrival of tenders, guiding

Launches from the great motor yachts as they pick up their owners and guests on the landing stage of the New York Yacht Club's station at Newport before the second race for the America's Cup on August 2, 1937. *Author's collection.*

guests to their point of debarkation," had been sold.[3] In its place was "a public landing pier with marinas and a bar."[4] Mary Cremmen, a *Boston Globe* correspondent, ventured into the watering hole and was surprised to see "a juke box where Vanderbilts and Astors sat with Oelrichs waiting for launches to take them to their 300-foot steam yachts."[5]

World War II had been a dramatic curtain call on the argosy of splendor whose time now seemed as distant as the Jurassic Age. Dunton and Cremmen were attempting to come to grips with the sea change that had followed.

Newport's belle époque of yachting had developed gradually over the better part of a century and reached its zenith between the world wars, an era that included the Roaring Twenties, Prohibition and the America's Cup Races of the 1930s. This introduction traces the emergence of Newport as the pastime's capital, while the chapters that follow profile some of the epoch's most colorful yachtsmen, their splendid craft and remarkable stories often involving the perils they faced in the age before electronic navigation. Drawn to the "City by the Sea," as the Rhode Island port was also known, by

Nattily attired Countess Alfonso Villa and corporate magnate H.E. Manville were among the glitterati preparing to leave the club's landing to see an America's Cup race on August 4, 1937. *Author's collection.*

their passion for yachting, many of these well-heeled sea dogs were captains of finance and industry who, along with their scions, would build their summer places, or "cottages," there, while others were content to remain aboard their floating palaces, yachting having always been something of a nomadic pursuit. The era of "extravagant magnificence" afloat was fleeting, but the names of many of its leading figures are still well known to us today and very much part of Newport's lore.

ORIGINS

Newport would be a cradle of many of the nation's recreational pursuits, but it was the passion for yachting, a generation before the appearance of tennis, golf and polo, that was to be an important catalyst for the nascent resort.[6]

It was aboard a schooner, anchored off the Battery at the foot of Manhattan on a July day in 1844, that a meeting took place that would have great consequence for Newport. Nine men had assembled to form the New York Yacht Club, and before the meeting adjourned, they had resolved to cruise to Newport a few days later. No sooner had the New York fleet, led by Commodore John C. Stevens's schooner *Gimcrack*, arrived than three yachts from Boston were bound for the Rhode Island port. The hub's squadron included Colonel William P. Winchester's celebrated schooner *Northern Light* and the Boston pilot schooner *Belle*, which had been chartered to the China trader and seasoned mariner Robert Bennet "Black Ben" Forbes, so named for a bush of dark hair he'd had as a young man. "Trials of speed" soon took place to the delight of the press, along with controversy over whether the centerboard craft, favored by the New Yorkers, were a match for the Bostonians' deep-keel yachts. Stevens, an illustrious turfman who had owned the great Thoroughbred Eclipse, offered a wager for a match between a New York pilot schooner and *Northern Light*, a challenge that was not accepted—but the stage had been set. The New York and Boston fleets would meet again. "Black Ben" joined the New York Yacht Club, and Newport was judged the perfect rendezvous. Its location and protected harbor were ideal, as was its easy access to Block Island Sound, a euphemism for the Atlantic Ocean, to be sure, but an ideal expanse of water for competitive sailing. By the mid-1850s, the City by the Sea would be a regular port-of-call on the New York Yacht Club's annual cruise and its first regatta off the port in 1854.

Ashore, the yachtsmen were sure to have frequented the resort's first large hotels, Ocean House and the Atlantic Hotel, both serendipitously appearing in 1844, with the latter being the venue for a ball held during the club's 1860 cruise. It was a Bostonian, David Sears, who would build the first cottage that can be associated with the yachting phenomenon in Newport. The Brahmin merchant, whose handsome granite, bow-front residence facing the Boston Common is today's Somerset Club, built Red Cross Cottage in 1844 in the district behind the Redwood Library. It is not known why Sears forsook Nahant, his previous summer colony north of Boston, for a new watering spot, but it likely was a reflection of his son's passionate interest in the nascent pastime. David Sears Jr. (1822–1874) had been part of the Boston contingent that had sailed down in 1844. Owner of the crack schooner *Brenda*, he had also joined the New York Yacht Club and would later be a founder and the second commodore of Marblehead's Eastern Yacht Club.

William Edgar, who was adept at both racing around the buoys and concocting Antigua rum punches, succeeded John C. Stevens as commodore of the New York Yacht Club and was the first of the New York tars to build a cottage in the late 1840s. Sunnyside, Edgar's McKim, Mead and White tidewater brick residence on Old Beach Road, not far from the Sears villa, replaced his earlier cottage in the 1880s.

The post–Civil War years brought more yachtsmen to the City by the Sea as new yacht clubs were formed. The Seawanhaka Yacht Club, from Oyster Bay on Long Island's North Shore, was the sponsor of the nation's first open Corinthian (amateur) regatta at Newport in 1874. Founded by young men who liked to "scrape, paint, rig, and sail their own boats," the club presented a $500 cup, receiving entries from half a dozen different yacht clubs.[7] Other yacht clubs' cruises were now bound for Newport as well, and Brooklyn's posh Atlantic Yacht Club and the New Haven Yacht Club sailed in during the 1882 season. The *New York Telegram* commented on the phenomenon that summer, reporting that "these aquatic picnics have become a staple amusement in late years with the principal yacht owners and their extensive circle of guests."[8]

It was during this era that maiden voyages of some of the nation's most celebrated yachts were also now bound for Newport. In 1869, Pierre Lorillard's younger brother George built the 130-foot schooner *Meteor*, subject of a glorious Currier & Ives lithograph, and got underway for the Rhode Island port after its launching in Brooklyn that June.[9] *Meteor* would remain in the nation's news after being lost later that year on shoals off

Newport's come-hither only magnified after the Civil War as an increasing number of
yachts and club cruises were drawn to the City by the Sea. *From* Harper's Weekly.

Cape Bon on the Mediterranean's Africa coast. The American consul at Tunis, rushing to the rescue on a chartered steamer, found Lorillard and his afterguard living well under tents made up from the yacht's sails and spars, along with the *Meteor*'s piano and store of spirits. Armed sentries drawn from the crew kept marauders at bay.

James Gordon Bennett Jr.

It would be a young yachtsman who had first sailed in at the age of sixteen at the helm of his own seventy-two-foot yacht who would not only help stimulate interest in his favorite pastime but also broaden the resort's appeal by introducing Newport to yet other recreational pursuits. James Gordon "Jamie" Bennett Jr., son of the publisher of the *New York Herald*, was the founder of the Newport Casino (1879–81) across Bellevue Avenue from his own cottage, Stone Villa.[10] The venue for the first thirty-four years of the U.S. Tennis Open, the handsome block-long facility designed by McKim, Mead and White would become the summer colony's social center. It offered not only tennis courts but also the amenities of a modern country club with dining, card and billiard rooms and a theater. The colorful Bennett, who introduced polo to America, also brought the game to Newport, where the first international match against the British would be played in 1880. On the water, he was a legend. Victor of the Great Ocean Race of 1866 (the first transatlantic race), and donor among other trophies of the Brenton Reef Challenge Cup for a race from Newport to Sandy Hook and back, he was the only yachtsman twice elected commodore of the New York Yacht Club.

Julius Chambers, the *Brooklyn Daily Eagle*'s distinguished journalist, recalled the halcyon morning in Newport in August 1870, when, just after graduating from Cornell, he first encountered Bennett. Invited to race aboard his storied schooner *Dauntless*, Chambers and a reporter from the *New York World* were headed out to the yacht in a launch when they observed a swimmer, far from the anchorage, moving rapidly through the water using the English stroke, in which the swimmer uses a breaststroke kick and butterfly arms. On reaching the yacht, the two guests were welcomed by the sailing master Samuel Samuels and surprised a few minutes later when the swimmer climbed a ladder and appeared, "robed in nature's pink morocco." Only after he extended a hand that "bore the ocean's chill" did they realize it was Bennett.[11] He was, Chambers wrote, "the enthusiasm of every seaman in the American pleasure navy," then at Newport.[12]

Among the first cottagers to see the advantages steam yachts held for rapid transit to the Ocean State, his flyer *Polynia* was launched in 1880, the year before William H. Osgood's *Stranger* amazed the public with his record nine hours from Newport, where he had breakfast, to New York, in time for dinner.[13] By 1906, when Willie K. Vanderbilt Jr. attempted a record run in his turbine-powered *Tarantula*, the passage was expected to take six hours. Peter Rouse would shave more than an hour off that time with his 225-foot *Winchester* in 1911.[14] Getting to Newport quickly would continue to be an obsession for the leisure class with the appearance of planing hulls for commuting yachts after World War I. Captured in celluloid

James Gordon "Jamie" Bennett Jr., publisher of the *New York Herald* and an avid yachtsman, introduced Newport to other pastimes, broadening the resort's appeal. *New York Yacht Club Archive.*

at the New York Yacht Club's Newport landing in the late 1930s was one such vessel that would have done it in under four. Charles S. Payson's streamlined *Saga*, a 70-foot machine-age expression built in 1935 at record cost for a boat of its length, had a pair of big twelve-cylinder Packards, fabulous marine engines that could push it along at forty-four knots but required a prodigious amount of petrol. Bound from Newport to Maine one year, Payson radioed ahead for fuel but was surprised on arrival to find a queue on the gas dock at Gloucester. Alerted by the call, the dock's creditors were patiently waiting.

Steam yachts could also be used for receptions on a grand scale, as Bennett and Caroline Astor, forerunners of such legendary twentieth-century entertainers as Sadie Jones and Henry Walters, would later demonstrate. Bennett's *Namouna*, launched in 1882, the largest steam yacht in the New York Yacht Club's fleet at the time of its construction, was certainly well suited for it, with McKim, Mead and White–designed interiors and glass and mosaics supplied in part by Louis Comfort Tiffany.[15] Great excitement surrounded the extravagant yacht's arrival from Europe in August 1884 and the grand reception aboard at Newport, to which Commodore Bennett invited all the yachtsmen and prominent cottagers. The *New York Times* reported:

Carriage after carriage rattled down the wharves, and their occupants were quickly on board steam launches, cutters and sailboats and transferred to the Namouna *which was looking her best. The mahogany and brass work were polished, and the engine room was as tidy as the sumptuously furnished saloons, chat room, dining room, etc. The craft was never in better trim and was admired by the distinguished throng of visitors. A New York orchestra was on board and furnished music for five hours. The collation was doubtless one of the most elaborate ever spread on board a ship, and the same can also be said of the floral display.*[16]

The guests would have observed a novelty on boarding. At a time when most yachts just dropped anchor at Newport, Bennett had one of the first moorings. The iron buoy he had built was six feet in diameter and attached to a self-clearing chain that led to a huge mushroom anchor he placed in Brenton's Cove. The timesaving device made it far easier to moor or get underway.[17]

Novelties would abound on the commodore's next yacht as well, the magnificent 314-foot G.L. Watson–designed *Lysistrata* built in 1900, the equal of any Gilded Age royal yacht, and outfitted with a Turkish bath and padded stall for an Alderney cow that provided for dairy needs. By that time, however, Bennett was an expatriate running his publishing empire by transatlantic cable. Nevertheless, *Lysistrata* was at Newport in June 1904; visitors would have seen that the yachtsman's fetish for owl motifs had reached a new height, presenting carved images of the birds set in mistletoe boughs on the bow and stern lit with electric eyes.[18]

OGDEN GOELET

It is interesting that the man who would have an even greater role in establishing Newport as the nation's yachting capital was not a commodore or even a racing man. Ogden Goelet (1851–1897), along with his brother, Robert, inherited an immense New York real estate fortune, established by forbears who were famous for their practice of never, or rarely, selling, and loved yachting. A prescient booster of the pastime, he foresaw the value of establishing an annual series and, in 1882, began to commission the magnificent silver presentation pieces, covered in the iconography of the sea, that were to be raced for each year off Newport. Created by the leading firms of Tiffany and Whiting Manufacturing, each Goelet cup was unique in design, exceptional in craftsmanship and extravagantly valued at $500 for the prize for sloops and $1,000 for schooners.

Thirty entries were received the first year, and interest in the competition was buoyed in the following years by extensive press coverage, *Harper's Weekly* illustrations and even images of the elaborate trophies, which fascinated the public. "The cliffs," the *New York Herald* reported in 1884, "were covered with spectators to see the races today,"[19] while the *Newport Mercury* described the "lively scene" a decade later, as the contenders got underway followed by "scores of other yachts, steamboats, tugs and catboats that follow as spectators."[20] On the fifth anniversary of the competition, the *New York Times* observed the Goelet Cup was coming "to be recognized as our national derby" and thought it "better worth winning than any other trophy offered for competition by American yachts."[21] By 1893, the paper offered even greater accolades, noting that the Goelet Cup had become the "blue ribbon of our aquatic contests" and that some of "the races for it have been among the most exciting and instructive that have ever taken place in our waters."[22] Profiles of two of the winners, Jesse Metcalf, a future U.S. senator from Rhode Island, and E.D. Morgan, owner of the invincible Herreshoff sloop *Gloriana*, appear within these pages.

Ogden would be on hand for the first thirteen seasons of the competition he sponsored, working with his first cousin and long-time commodore of the New York Yacht Club E.T. Gerry to ensure its success. When fog delayed the races one year, he characteristically kept spirits high by hosting a "magnificent entertainment" aboard his schooner, the *Norseman*, for "all the yachtsmen and their guests."[23]

Gerry's aptly named 173-foot flagship *Electra*, the first steam yacht with electric lighting, thanks to the involvement of Thomas Edison, followed the races with dignitaries and correspondents aboard. The *Illustrated American* hailed Ogden's cousin as a "great friend of the press"[24] in his promotion of the regatta, and that was probably something of an understatement. Gerry's biographer Shelley L. Dowling noted that one reporter, A.G. McVey of the *Boston Herald*, availed himself of the commodore's hospitality for twenty-three consecutive years![25]

In 1889, Goelet recognized something else that was required to facilitate yachting in Newport, where the carriages of the well-heeled attempting to board launches crossed paths with the wagons of fishmongers and ship chandlers. A dedicated and suitable landing facility on the waterfront was needed to create a link between the yachts in the harbor and fashionable

Commodore E.T. Gerry's aptly named *Electra*, the first steam yacht with electric lights thanks to the involvement of Thomas Edison, is seen here at Newport in 1888 as the New York Yacht Club's fleet gets underway. Just ahead of *Electra* is the 1885 America's Cup defender, *Puritan*, and over Goat Island some of the yachts are already rounding Fort Adams. *Section of a panorama by Henry G. Peabody, Detroit Collection, Library of Congress.*

Ogden Goelet and his brother Robert purchased part of Sayer's Wharf in 1889, building and leasing an attractive shore station to the New York Yacht Club. *George Grantham Bain Collection, Library of Congress.*

Bellevue Avenue. Along with his brother, Robert, he purchased part of Sayer's Wharf, which was then leased to the New York Yacht Club, and had an attractive shore station (later known as Station No. 6) constructed.[26] It was described in 1891 "as a little building where one can have his letters sent and his parcels delivered for the yacht" and where "the yachtsman can wait for his gig to come ashore" or make use of two verandas "where one can sit and 'look lazy at the sea.'"[27]

These improvements did not go unrecognized. That fall, the *New York Times* noted:

> *The greatest races of the past seasons, which go to the credit of the New York Yacht Club, occurred during its squadron cruise at Newport. The club having established a clubhouse at Newport for the convenience of members that are doing much to make Newport a popular yachting rendezvous, is drifting, to all appearance, into the way of giving races off Newport in preference to having them over its regular course in and around New York Bay.*[28]

A comparison of dates of election to the New York Yacht Club and cottage starts in Newport indicates the effect the change of playgrounds was having ashore. While only a handful of members had erected or acquired villas in the 1860s and '70s, at least two dozen would do so in the final decades of the nineteenth century. By 1912, the *Newport Directory* listed at least fifty-eight members of the New York Yacht Club or their widows as villa owners.[29] The yachting phenomenon contributed to the privatization of Newport as it diverged from Saratoga Springs and other American resorts that remained reliant on hotels.

Ogden had played a great role in Newport's ascendancy as the capitol of American yachting, but both he and his brother were gone, claimed by heart disease, before the twentieth century dawned. His demise in 1897 also brought to an end the competition for which he had presented the cups, but providentially, after the lapse of a year, John Jacob Astor came forward to continue the tradition begun by Ogden. Astor Cups have been raced for ever since, except at times of war. Among the Astor winners profiled in this book are August Belmont, J. Pierpont Morgan, E.D. Morgan, Harry Payne Whitney, Cornelius "Neily" Vanderbilt and the man who won the competition an astounding nine times, Harold S. "Mike" Vanderbilt. Tessie Oelrichs's famous 1904 Bal Blanc at Rosecliff was to celebrate the Astor Cup that year and featured an ersatz fleet of white ships floating in the sea.

Packed boats and palatial yachts vied for the best vantage points to see the first race in the 1937 America's Cup match. *Author's collection.*

The table was largely set by the turn of the twentieth century for Newport's ascendancy as the capital of America's yachting. The Bermuda Race, the nation's oldest regularly scheduled ocean race, finally established Newport as its starting point in 1936, but there was still one cup missing: the "auld mug," the America's Cup, the oldest trophy in international sports, which had been competed for off New York since 1870. However, given the sporadic nature of challenge cups between 1903 and 1930, there had been only one match, held in 1920. While many American yachtsmen felt that Newport, with its better sailing conditions, would be the ideal venue, Sir Thomas Lipton demurred. "Sir Tea" preferred New York, seeing those waters as neutral and where it was more likely that the public would see the match. In 1920, Lipton had his druthers when the races were again held off New York, but in 1930, he did not, and Newport finally became the venue for yachting's Holy Grail. A record fleet of pleasure craft descended on Newport that summer to see the greatest spectacle the sport has to offer, and they would return en masse in '34 and '37. Writing for the *Chicago Tribune* in 1934, Nancy Randolph tried to explain to her midwestern readership just how big the America's

Cup had gotten. The "exodus of notables" from the Big Apple headed for Newport to see the races was so great, "Every yacht in commission has weighed anchor and gone to join the galaxy of watercraft" off the Rhode Island port.[30]

While it may seem curious to us that these floating festivals were going on during the Great Depression, they were, in reality, the antidote, along with sports in general, to bank failures, deflation and a stock market that, by 1932, was worth a tenth of what it had been in 1929. For those who could afford to keep their yachts in commission, it was the last stand of the "extravagant magnificence" of Newport's yachtsmen between the wars.

1

WILLIAM VINCENT ASTOR

(1891–1959)

On a frigid April night in 1912, Colonel John Jacob "Jack" Astor helped his pregnant wife, Madeleine, aboard one of the *Titanic*'s lifeboats filled with women and children, reassured her he would see her in the morning and was heard asking the ship's officer, overseeing the launching, the boat's number so he could find her again. The colonel, a Spanish American war veteran and the *Titanic*'s wealthiest first-class passenger, was last seen on the starboard bridge wing smoking a cigarette in the moments before the great liner slid toward its doom. The tragedy, which rewrote the scripts of so many lives, caught young Vincent Astor, the colonel's twenty-year-old son from his first marriage, in his second year at Harvard. Leaving college to preside over his family's real estate empire, Vincent's first task was making the arrangements for his father's funeral. Eight days after the sinking, the cable ship *MacKay-Bennett* recovered Astor's remains. Floating upright in a life belt, the colonel's corpse was identified by the initials on the label of his suit, which contained a small fortune in currency and a gold pocket watch. The timepiece was claimed by his adoring son, and Vincent would carry the watch for the rest of his life. Ferncliff, the Astors' estate on the Hudson River; Beechwood, their Bellevue Avenue cottage in Newport; *Noma*, his father's steam yacht; and a $90 million fortune would also pass to Vincent. Yet it was his father's great affinity for the sea and marine engineering that would prove to be the greatest inheritance. "I like the sea," Vincent would say in 1928, "nothing appeals to me more. In fact, if I had been born under different circumstances and did not have other

Right: Vincent Astor at the New York Yacht Club's landing in Newport before the 1932 Astor Cup. He would serve as the club's commodore between 1928 and 1930. *Author's collection*.

Below: The elegant 262-foot steam yacht *Noma* would become Vincent's as result of his father's demise, and he would serve aboard it as an ensign when it was in naval service as the USS *Noma* during World War I. *Author's collection*.

matters to command my attention, I would like nothing better than to be a nautical engineer."[31]

The Astors' yachting saga began with Jack's pleasure-seeking father, William B. Astor Jr. (1830–1892), who preferred his schooner, *Ambassadress*, to the social scene orchestrated by his wife, Caroline, the "Mrs. Astor," acknowledged queen of Newport and New York society. He would spend increasing amounts of time in Florida waters aboard his 146-foot yacht. Built in 1877 with a center board for southern cruising, the *Ambassadress* was the largest sailing yacht up to that time. Caroline Astor went so far as to tell Bessie Lehr, wife of the social arbiter, with whom she had established the society list known as the 400, that the sea air was good for her husband: "It is a great pity I am such a bad sailor, for I should so much enjoy accompanying him. As it is, I have never even set foot on the yacht."[32]

Caroline's yachting epiphany occurred, however, when the schooner reached Newport. Below decks, the posh yacht was "finished in walnut, maple, mahogany, and cherry" and had a large salon, upholstered furniture and an "elegant bronze chandelier,"[33] the perfect stage with all the requisites for Caroline to advance her social agenda. The *Brooklyn Daily Eagle* reported in August 1879 that "Mrs. William Astor gave a brilliant entertainment aboard the *Ambassadress* while at the Rhode Island port for two hundred guests."[34]

In the 1880s, William Astor was swept up in the craze for steam yachts and sold the *Ambassadress*. It sailed on, though, for many years as a yacht, then as a Boston fisherman and, after being re-rigged as a brigantine, ended its days as a packet trading between France and Madagascar.

The first of the Astors' *Nourmahals*, meaning "light of harem," was built in 1884 at the Harlan & Hollingsworth yard in Wilmington, Delaware. The longest steam yacht in the New York Yacht Club's fleet at the time, the 233-foot vessel was a schooner rigged with three masts so that it could "carry sufficient sail for propulsion in the event of an accident to the machinery."[35] A prudent precaution, as it turned out, as the accident-prone floating palace would have its share of mishaps. While under charter to James Waterbury in 1892, the year William Astor died, it sustained damage after being brushed by an unknown steamer on a dark night off New London. The following year, after passing to Jack, *Nourmahal* went ashore off Rhode Island during a gale and required three tugs to pull it free. Then it ran aground up the Hudson near Poughkeepsie, punching a hole in its bottom and resulting in the dismissal of the captain for carelessness. However, the season's coup de grace did not occur until October for the craft that the press would dub the "unlucky yacht."[36] Steaming down the Hudson under "a full head of steam," bound for the America's Cup races off Sandy Hook with Astor on the bridge, *Nourmahal* slammed into the Pennsylvania Railroad's ferry *Washington*, which had just left its pier at Jersey City.[37] The yacht, which lost its bowsprit, had failed to heed the ferry's whistles.

Nonetheless, the travails of Jack Astor's first season as owner were not repeated. The capable crew he assembled traveled far, often with young Vincent and his tutor aboard, and rode out a Caribbean hurricane in 1909.

At Newport, the parade of prominent guests to board the yacht, often to observe regattas, included such luminaries as Theodore Roosevelt's daughter Alice. When Ogden Goelet—donor of the cups for the most important annual competition off Newport—died in 1897, Jack offered to take his place as the provider of the trophies. The Astor Cup series continues to this day.

In 1910, Astor acquired an even larger yacht. The elegant 262-foot *Noma* had been designed by Clinton Crane for W.B. Leeds, the "tin plate king," in 1902. It had twin stacks, a beautiful sheer line and was faster and better appointed than Astor's previous yacht. Desirous of both speed and luxury, goals difficult to reconcile, Leeds had driven Crane crazy during the design process with constant change orders. The usual enamel tubs specified by the naval architect weren't good enough for his difficult client, who insisted on large, custom-made porcelain tubs. Things went further off course when they got to the paneling for the cabin. Leeds turned to the architects of his Fifth Avenue residence, Hunt and Hunt, whose heavy interior woodwork for the yacht went well beyond what had been called for in the original plans. "I feel that every time a house architect is brought on shipboard," lamented Crane, "he feels it necessary to include dolphins, starfish, scallop shells, and all kinds of marine growth to emphasize the fact that this is a ship."[38] Luckily, *Noma* passed the requisite speed trial on completion despite the added weight, although Crane observed that "she was below her designed lines as a result."[39] *Noma* was already known to Newport before Astor obtained it, as Leeds summered there, first leasing and then buying Frederick Vanderbilt's Rough Point. A stroke in 1905 left the tin plate king partially paralyzed, and he died three years later at forty-seven. The colonel's enjoyment of the posh pleasure craft would even be shorter, and in 1912, *Noma* became Vincent's first yacht. Newport must have been relieved the following April when *Noma* reappeared. Vincent, accompanied by Hermann Oelrichs Jr., went ashore to inspect Beechwood, which he opened for the season.

When the United States entered World War I in 1917, Vincent, who had been commissioned an ensign in the Naval Reserve, loaned the yacht to the Navy and actually served on board the USS *Noma*. Part of the famous Breton Patrol of armed American yachts engaged in antisubmarine duty, the USS *Noma* was in hot engagements with a number of German submarines. Ensign Astor, who was promoted to lieutenant in 1918, later served on the USS *Aphrodite*, Colonel Oliver H. Payne's yacht, which was also part of the patrol, and returned to the United States in 1919 aboard the captured German sub *U-117*.

By war's end, *Noma* had seen a lot of water pass under its keel, and the aging steam yacht was facing obsolescence in the face of the great economy, in space, crew and cost inherent in Rudolph Diesel's invention of an efficient combustion engine.

Vincent sold *Noma* in 1921 and built his first motor yacht, *Nourmahal* (II), designed by Cox and Stevens. Although only 160 feet overall, the state-of-the-art diesel-powered yacht was both luxurious and versatile, the perfect craft for Vincent to access both Ferncliff and Beechwood from the New York Yacht Club's station on the East River at the foot of 23rd Street in Manhattan. Gheradi Davis, a member of the club's race committee who was aboard *Nourmahal* (II) for the 1922 NYYC Cruise, thought the yacht was "very comfortable" and remarked, "Her main cabin was a superb room paneled in beautiful wood and not the least attractive decoration was a very clever map of Long Island Sound and the Cape Cod waters, spreading across the after end of the room and drawn and colored like a sixteenth-century map."[40]

As *Nourmahal* (II) was less than suitable for the around-the-world cruising Astor was contemplating by the late 1920s, he would only have it for less than a decade. In service in the Canadian navy during World War II as the HMCS *Otter*, it was lost in a fire off Halifax in 1941.

Vincent's next *Nourmahal* (III) was a fitting finale to a half century of Astor yacht building and his flagship as commodore of the New York Yacht Club (1928–30.) "'Super-Yacht' Era Here with New Astor Craft," James C. Young headlined his three-column description of the vessel in the *New York Times* on its arrival in New York in 1928. It wasn't that the *Nourmahal* (III), which had been built by Krupp Works in Germany, was so long at 263 feet, 10 inches, but its appearance was markedly different. With a plumb stem rather than a clipper bow and a generous beam, the yacht had more the look of a small ocean liner. Astor had expressed his preference for a "steamship yacht" with Theodore E. Ferris during the design phase, and the Cox and Stevens naval architect gave him just what he desired.[41]

Above: The Krupp-built, 263-foot,10-inch *Nourmahal* (III), a fitting finale to a half century of Astor yacht building, had a plumb stern and the steamship-like appearance Vincent Astor preferred. *Author's collection.*

Left: A dry dock painter stands under one of *Nourmahal's* (III) huge propellers as he looks up at the double-bottomed hull. *The Edwin Levick Collection, Mariners' Museum and Park, 96428.*

Nourmahal's (III) library was finished with waxed and pegged Norwegian pine. *The Edwin Levick Collection, Mariners' Museum and Park, 96434.*

Powered by a pair of 3,200-horsepower diesels, boasting a cruising range of 19,000 miles and constructed with multiple watertight bulkheads, the massive double-bottomed vessel was certainly seaworthy and could take its owner comfortably to any part of the world. Reporter Young found its interiors spacious and cheerful, commenting favorably on the library, which had been finished with waxed and pegged Norwegian pine, and the dining salon—its mahogany table sat eighteen. Yet it was the engine room that truly amazed, built on two levels, the hold having a depth of 22 feet and filled with engines, generators, pumps for air circulation and apparatus for a dozen other tasks.

Franklin Delano Roosevelt, Astor's great friend, near neighbor on the Hudson and relative—his half brother, James, had married Vincent's aunt Helen Astor—was also impressed. On seeing *Nourmahal* (III), he joked that he would have to increase taxes on the rich.[42] With FDR's election in 1932, *Nourmahal* began a new role as the president's favored yacht. Herbert Hoover decommissioned the *Mayflower* three years earlier, and the only presidential yacht during Roosevelt's first term was the 104-foot *Sequoia*, a wooden houseboat that didn't hold a candle to Astor's magnificent oceangoing vessel. Vincent made *Nourmahal* available to the president for five cruises, well chronicled by the press, in the mid-1930s.

"By going aboard a private yacht, he gets the seclusion he seeks," noted the *United States News* in 1934, "no reporters, no mail, no telegrams, and no callers and job seekers."[43] FDR agreed, "It's the only place I can get away from people, telephones, and uniforms,"[44] although a destroyer always followed in the yacht's wake.

Seclusion doesn't seem to have been the only motivation. He was there for all the fun in '34 for the America's Cup match off Newport. The competing skippers, Harold "Mike" Vanderbilt and T.O.M. Sopwith, were received on board. Flying the president's flag, *Nourmahal* was at the center of the spectator fleet, viewing the international races. Roosevelt, dressed in a gray suit, was easy to distinguish, as Astor and most of his afterguard were attired in their blue yachting jackets and white duck pants.

FDR would take five cruises aboard *Nourmahal* (III) in the mid-1930s, and the president was aboard to observe the America's Cup Races off Newport in 1934. Here he is seen at the left with Kermit Roosevelt (*center*) and Vincent Astor (*right*) as they leave the yacht in 1933. *Author's collection.*

FDR's inner circle, friends and relatives, were his shipmates for most of these cruises. In addition to Vincent, his son James Roosevelt, cousin Kermit Roosevelt, Judge Frederic Kernochan and the well-heeled New Yorker William Rhinelander Stewart were regulars. The group provided not only companionship but also a sounding board for the president on current affairs, and he soon had another mission for the *Nourmahal*. Concerned about Japanese intentions in the Pacific, Roosevelt helped facilitate Vincent and Kermit's cruise aboard the yacht to the Marshall Islands in 1938. Ostensibly a scientific expedition aimed at collecting marine specimens, the voyage was really an undercover operation to gather intelligence on Tokyo's activities and bases in that theater.

Nourmahal returned to Newport for the 1937 match for the America's Cup with the president's wife aboard and again in 1940, but the following year, both the yacht and its owner would be swept up by the twentieth century's greatest conflict. In August 1941, Astor, a commander in the Naval Reserve, turned *Nourmahal* over to the Coast Guard for use as a weather station ship, requesting he not be assigned to serve aboard. Involved in convoy planning and counterespionage work ashore, he would rise to the rank of captain by war's end. Later transferred to the Navy, the USS *Nourmahal* escorted convoys between New York and Guantanamo Bay and served as flagship of the commander of the Eastern Sea Frontier. Decommissioned in 1946, *Nourmahal* was offered by the Navy to President Truman as the Presidential Yacht, but he turned it down, reportedly because he considered the yacht too large.[45]

Joining the government's mothball fleet on Virginia's James River in 1948, the forsaken flagship would remain there for sixteen long years. Once one of the world's most famous yachts, *Nourmahal* was now moored in ignominy in the ghost fleet of forgotten freighters, tankers, buoy tenders and sundry naval vessels that stretched for five miles along the river. The Maritime Administration, the government agency charged with selling surplus ships, attempted to find a buyer who would pay more than scrap value. The bids received, however, did not exceed $62,000 for the super-yacht that Astor had paid at least $600,000 to build and outfit.[46] Then, in 1964, five years after Vincent Astor's death, the *Nourmahal* was finally sold.

Texas oilman John Mecom thought it could be an attraction for the vast Flamingo Isles development and marina complex he planned across the bay from Galveston. He purchased the monorail from the 1964 World's Fair to link the many features he planned, which would include a floating hotel, the *Nourmahal*. After it was towed to Texas City, Texas,

The famous yacht capsized and sank following a fire aboard at Texas City, Texas, in 1964. *Author's collection.*

for the overhaul, a fire thought to have been ignited by cleaning solvents broke out aboard. Responding firemen had to pour so much water on the flames that the curtain came down on the famous yacht, which capsized and sank.[47]

2

GEORGE F. BAKER JR.

(1878–1937)

In 1929, George F. Baker Jr. took possession of his magnificent, new turboelectric motor yacht at a pier on Manhattan's West Side. Pleased with what he saw aboard *Viking* (II), a 272-foot, steel-hulled beauty, he told the captain to get underway for Newport before turning in for the night. On awakening the next morning, he marveled at how quiet the engines had been—it was beyond all his expectations. But on stepping out of his cabin, he was surprised to see the towers of Manhattan. There had been a mechanical problem, and the *Viking* was still at the pier on the West Side.[48]

While he would never have a villa on Bellevue Avenue, Baker did get to Newport frequently. In *Viking*, he had what Bill Robinson once described as a "full-blown estate gone to sea,"[49] which was all this commodore of the New York Yacht Club required. If terra firma ever beckoned, his sister Florence Baker Loew's Stoneacre, a Bellevue showplace with grounds by Frederick Law Olmsted, was not far distant.

George was the son of the "Sphinx of Wall Street," the legendary financier and ally of J.P. Morgan, who co-founded and chaired for decades the First National Bank of the City of New York, precursor to today's Citibank. The taciturn and difficult senior Baker, in the only interview he ever granted a journalist, cautioned, "Everyone should reduce his talk, I don't talk because silence is the secret of success."[50]

George Jr. assumed the reins of the great commercial bank on his father's death in 1931 but took a different tack through life. A *Brooklyn Daily Eagle* profile in 1916 found young Baker reticent to talk about himself

George F. Baker Jr.
aboard his steam yacht
Viking, circa 1920.
Author's collection.

but energetic, unassuming, popular and thoughtful. "He lives between his desk, his yacht, and his family," the paper observed, and when he leaves the bank "generally boards his yacht, the *Viking* or his sloop, the *Ventura*."[51] His generosity was often demonstrated, Sherman Hoyt recalled, noting that with Prohibition in full swing, there wasn't much aboard *Resolute* or its tender with which to celebrate their America's Cup victory over *Shamrock IV* until Baker "pulled up alongside" with his commuter, *Little Viking*, "well stocked with champagne."[52] When Baker was elected commodore of the New York Yacht Club in 1914 at thirty-six, the *Eagle* noted that he "commands the *Viking* personally" and was a qualified mariner in positions ranging from able seaman to captain, should he ever lose his fortune and have to "support himself and his family before the mast."[53]

There would be two *Vikings*, both designed by Theodore Wells. The first was a 180-foot Wilmington-built steam yacht Baker owned for twenty years. It was his flagship when commodore, and he spent so much time aboard that even his engagement to Edith Kane was announced by letters the young couple dated from the yacht. The financier's fleet also included the 72-foot

The magnificent 272-foot, turboelectric *Viking* (II), also designed by Theodore D. Wells, was launched in 1929. *The Mariners' Museum and Park.*

sloop *Ventura*, a New York Fifty with which he won the King's Cup in 1915, and his commuter, *Little Viking*. Stepping aboard the latter each morning at Viking's Cove, his country house on Long Island, Baker would dress as the yacht raced toward Manhattan, his valet having laid out his attire for the day. It's not known if the yachtsman ever attempted, at Brenton's Cove, what he was fond of doing on a calm night at Viking's Cove: having his crew project films from the bridge of *Viking* onto the main sail of *Ventura*, moored nearby. This was the probable cause of an over-served neighbor claiming she had seen Indians chasing Tom Mix, the cowboy movie star, down the Long Island Sound.

At Newport, Baker was a yachting booster, donating cups, accompanying, aboard *Viking*, the first Bermuda Race to start from the port and as an America's Cup syndicate member. However, his greatest contribution to the pastime would be ashore. When the New York Yacht Club's 1890 Newport Station was judged to be inadequate, he was behind extensive improvements in 1915 and '16, which included a new clubhouse, additional property and the construction of a substantial pier and landing stages extending into the harbor, facilities which were to prove essential in support of the growing interest in the pastime and the arrival, in 1930, of the America's Cup

Baker would rebuild the New York Yacht Club's Newport Station, pier and landing stages at his own expense. Seen here during the 1930 America's Cup, members and their guests await tenders that will carry them to their yachts. *Author's collection*.

competition. All of the improvements were made at Baker's expense and donated to the yacht club.

In 1937, with the business climate improving, the financier thought the time was right for an around-the-world cruise aboard *Viking* (II). He reached Fuji Island with friends and his son, George, where he became stricken with appendicitis. A mid-ocean operation undertaken by Baker's personal physician, Dr. Alfred Ambler, and a surgeon from a Canadian Pacific liner bound from Auckland to Vancouver, was thought to have been successful. A few hours after the vessels had parted, however, the patient's condition worsened. Receiving word of the medical emergency, the Coast Guard at Honolulu, some 500 miles away, dispatched the cutter *Taney*, with Dr. D.J. Zaugg and nurses aboard. Serums that could not be collected before it got underway were air dropped at sea by a Navy plane. Dr. Zaugg, on boarding the *Viking*, gave Baker a blood transfusion. As the story hit the nation's morning papers, Edith Baker, who had been in New York, began an epic 5,500-mile flight to Honolulu, through unsettled weather, the last leg by a Pan-American clipper. Mrs. Baker arrived in time to be at her husband's side, but he died the next morning of peritonitis.

Acquired by the U.S. Navy in 1940, *Viking* (II) was converted at the Boston Navy Yard to the patrol gunboat USS *St. Augustine*. *U.S. National Archives, Bureau of Ships Collections, 19-N-24215.*

Norman Woolworth purchased the *Viking* the following year, but the yacht was acquired by the Navy late in 1940 and converted at Boston to the patrol gunboat USS *St. Augustine*. Clarence Michalis remembered serving on board in the summer of '41 off Massachusetts as a midshipman in the Harvard Naval ROTC program. Returning from a short cruise and unsure of their whereabouts in the fog, the captain decided to anchor. A launch was lowered to reconnoiter for government marks, and then through a break in the haze, Michalis could see the shore and something he recognized. It was a pavilion at Manchester-by-the-Sea, where he had been to a debutante's party the previous summer. Summoning the courage, the young man approached the captain and navigator on the bridge, who were bent over a chart, "Sir, I think I know where we are." Michalis also recalled that the comfortable and spacious yacht-turned-warship appeared to have been built with little in the way of bulkheads, as below decks, you could easily look from bow to stern.[54] Three years later while on convoy duty off Cape May, New Jersey, on a frigid January night in 1944, the USS *St. Augustine* was rammed by the tanker *Camas Meadows* and foundered in just five minutes. Of the 145 sailors aboard the armed yacht, just 30 survived.

3

AUGUST BELMONT JR.

(1853–1924)

August Belmont Jr., the trusted middle son of the great banker who would take over August Belmont & Company after his father's death in 1890, was an accomplished financier and a passionate sportsman. "Augie," who was often the first to see opportunity, founded the IRT, New York's first subway, and built the Cape Cod Canal and the nation's greatest racetrack, Belmont Park.

As a sportsman, he was principally an equestrian, playing polo, fox hunting and riding in amateur races. He was also a founder of Long Island's Meadow Brook Hunt, where his friend E.D. Morgan was master of the hounds in the 1880s. As a turfman, he served as chairman of the Jockey Club, bred 129 American Stakes winners, including the legendary Man O' War, and probably did more to advance the interests of this pastime at the turn of the twentieth century than anyone else. Hence, it's a bit surprising that Augie could find time for yachting, but this was certainly the case. Newport, the town his mother, Caroline Perry Belmont, so loved and where his illustrious grandfather Commodore Matthew C. Perry, who opened Japan to Western trade, was born, would be the venue.[55]

Margarita, Belmont's 46-foot sloop built in 1889, was followed two years later by *Mineola*, a 61-foot cutter, not to be confused with his luxurious private subway car of the same name. Both yachts were designed by Edward Burgess and built by Lawley, and he would also own the steam yacht *Ituna*. However, in 1897, Belmont was elected rear commodore of the New York Yacht Club and become involved in larger undertakings,

August Belmont Jr. and his wife, the British actress Eleanor Robson. *Photograph from the Nina Herald Webber Cape Cod Canal Collection, courtesy of Historic New England.*

commissioning the first of the Newport Seventies in 1900, the 105-foot sloops built by Herreshoff that were 70 feet on the waterline. *Mineola* (II) would soon be followed by H.B. Duryea and H.P. Whitney's *Yankee*, Cornelius Vanderbilt's *Rainbow* and W.K. Vanderbilt Jr.'s *Virginia*. "On the tide succeeding that on which *Mineola* was launched" at Bristol, the *New York Times* reported another Belmont vessel, "an elaborate steam yacht," which the financier's son Morgan christened *Scout*, "slid down the ways."[56] Designed as a tender for the powerless Newport Seventy *Scout*, the lightly built flyer could also be used for commuting and was third in the parade of vessels that opened the Cape Canal. And, while Belmont characteristically complained about the yacht's performance to Captain Nat Herreshoff, the "Wizard of Bristol" had the last word, observing that the speed attained during trials had, to his knowledge, not been surpassed by an anthracite-burning vessel of its size.[57]

Mineola (II), Belmont's 105-foot Newport Seventy built by Herreshoff and launched in 1906. *Library of Congress.*

Belmont also headed the *Constitution* syndicate that successfully defended the America's Cup in 1900 against Lipton's *Shamrock II* and was, again, a participant in 1903 when *Reliance* was chosen over *Constitution* after the defense trials.

In an age when the management of yachts was still largely left to professionals, it's hard to know to what degree Belmont was at the helm of his own craft. A press account of *"Mineola's* First Sail," however, noted that Captain Wringer "had the tiller a good part of the time"[58] and appears to have remained there in the races that followed.

Working for the financier must have been a challenge, as the often discontent Augie never seemed to be at peace with himself. His mother once remarked when he didn't get his way, "perhaps if you had a piece of the moon it would all be the same."[59] Quick to anger and, at times, narcissistic, he was famous for his dustups. One incident that revealed his dark side

Above: *Scout*, Belmont's Herreshoff flyer, was used as both a tender for *Mineola* (II) and a commuter. *Mystic Seaport Museum, Rosenfeld Collection Y.1984.187.278.*

Left: Harry Houdini, the celebrated illusionist, pictured here in New York in 1912, the same year he performed his overboard box escape stunt from the stern of the *Scout* for a Belmont lawn party at Newport. *Author's collection.*

occurred in 1883 on a Long Island train platform when he was approached by the father of a fourteen-year-old boy who had been trampled by one of his polo ponies. Belmont called the man, who was seeking payment of a twenty-five-dollar medical bill for his son, a "dead cur" and struck him over the head with his cane. The story appeared in the *New York Times* the next day under the headline "Young Belmont's Rage."[60]

As popular as he was difficult, Belmont's wife, the glamorous English actress Eleanor Robson, was a welcomed presence in the summer colony and a gracious hostess at the Belmonts' cottage, By The Sea. During the 1912 season, they hosted a large lawn party at which Harry Houdini, the celebrated illusionist, performed. The *Scout* was moored just off shore, and Augie took Houdini out to the yacht for his final act. Bound, handcuffed and locked in a box, the magician was lowered over the side as the Belmonts' guests, including J.P. Morgan and the German ambassador, "stood on the shore watching breathlessly," as Eleanor recalled in her memoirs.[61] To the relief of all, a minute later, Houdini reappeared on the surface, and the party was judged a great success.

4

JOHN R. DREXEL

(1862–1935)

The Drexel brothers quickly departed the business world following the death of their father, Anthony J. Drexel. The Philadelphia banker, one of the great titans of nineteenth-century finance, founded Drexel, Morgan & Company in 1871, a precursor to J.P. Morgan & Company, and was a mentor to his junior partner, J. Pierpont Morgan.

John Rozet Drexel and his younger brothers, A.J. "Tony" Drexel Jr.—who had been made a partner of his father's firm and was thought to be the heir apparent—and George W.C. Drexel, publisher of Philadelphia's *Public Ledger*, happily abandoned their endeavors to focus on yachting, Europe and society. The Drexel firm issued an announcement in young Tony's case, that he, at twenty-nine, was no longer interested in assuming the "responsibilities which are attached to the business" and "is fond of life in the society he adorns."[62]

George's 275-foot steam yacht *Alcedo* was the first American vessel lost during World War I while on Navy duty with the Breton Patrol. A.J. Drexel Jr. would have three magnificent steam yachts, all named *Margarita* for his wife, Margarita Armstrong Drexel, but apparently not enough to save the bon vivant's marriage, which ended in a bitter and much-publicized divorce in 1917. The first of the *Margaritas* would become well known in Newport after it was purchased by Henry Walters in 1899 and renamed *Narada*.

It was John R. Drexel who became the Newport cottager, acquiring Fairholme, which had been designed in 1870 by Philadelphians Fairman Rogers and Frank Furness and built at Ochre Point. John and his extravagant

John and Alice Drexel pictured at Cannes in 1927. *Drexel University Archives*.

wife, Alice Troth Drexel, would own Fairholme for more than three decades, adding a ballroom for their daughter's debut and transforming the Queen Anne cottage into a handsomely furnished showplace on par with their posh Horace Trumbauer–designed townhouse at 1 East 62nd Street in Manhattan. In short, the Gilded Age requisites for the socially ambitious Alice to enter the contest for social supremacy in Newport, along with a reported $200,000 John put at her disposal for dinner parties and entertaining, were all at Alice's fingertips.[63]

Advantage at sea was also secured by Drexel's purchase of *Sultana*, one of the most lavishly outfitted steam yachts of its day. Designed by the highly regarded J. Beaver Webb and built in Brooklyn by Handren & Robins in 1889 for a New York merchant, *Sultana* had all the amenities of the best floating palaces. The *New York Times* reported that below deck, the main saloon was "furnished in quartered oak, decorated in cream, gold, and blue after the Italian Renaissance period."[64] The 187-foot schooner-rigged steam yacht would become a common sight in the Newport anchorage.

Although a member of the New York Yacht Club, John was never "a yachting enthusiast," and acquaintances commented that he "seemed to be a man without hobbies or avocations."[65] Alice, it would appear, more than made up for her husband's lack of direction and was also the force behind the parties aboard *Sultana* and their annual cruise abroad. The best account

Sultana, the Drexels' 187-foot schooner-rigged steam yacht designed by the highly regarded J. Beaver Webb, while anchored on the Hudson River in 1897. *Detroit Publishing Company Collection, Library of Congress.*

of these excursions to European waters in the 1890s from the Norwegian fjords to the Riviera is found in the diary of one of their stewards, William F. Rasmussen, who spent twelve years aboard *Sultana*. At Tromso, Norway, one season, they encountered Kaiser Wilhelm II on the imperial yacht SMY *Hohenzollern*, which sent one of its launches over to ask if the Kaiser might visit. An invitation was extended with enthusiasm, and the *Sultana*'s crew got to work, making sure everything was shipshape and Bristol fashion. At the appointed hour, all hands were lined up at the gangway in dress whites, the stewards in white jackets with silk straps and the yacht's captain in a Prince Albert frock. Drexel, on the other hand, was attired in what appeared to be an admiral's uniform, awash in gold braids, which Rasmussen felt made him look like a Manhattan doorman. To the amazement of all, the Kaiser was piped aboard casually attired in nothing but a yachting jacket with black buttons. Over a glass of port from Napoleon's cellar, Rasmussen recalled, Drexel told the Kaiser he was troubled by gout, occasioning the emperor to send over a case of Mosel he thought would be therapeutic.[66]

With the outbreak of the Spanish-American War in the spring of 1898, while the Drexels' yacht was in the Mediterranean, the Associated Press reported on March 28 that Spain had just acquired the *Giralda*, the swift steam yacht of Colonel Harry McCalmont, the British sportsman. Built at Glasgow four years before, under the supervision of the British admiralty, it was capable of mounting eight guns and was currently carrying pairs of Maxim and Hotchkiss machine guns. The thought of an armed *Giralda*, already at Barcelona, preying on American yachts and merchant ships, was a real concern. In May, the British steamer *Noreham* witnessed a Spanish warship firing on a fleeing American merchant man near Gibraltar, and the *Sultana*, which had been pursued by a gunboat, sought refuge at Marseilles. The Drexels' captain John G. Potter reported to the press it would remain there until after the war because a suspicious telegram had been received by a yacht agent asking whether the American yacht was in port. Similar telegrams had been sent to determine the whereabouts of other American yachts, and the *Giralda*, Potter explained, which was capable of twenty-two knots, could easily overtake the *Sultana*.[67]

Effectively blockaded in Marseilles, Captain Potter used the time well, having the *Sultana* thoroughly overhauled, and when the short war was concluded, he steamed for home. The *Brooklyn Daily Eagle* noted its arrival in May 1899: "A great many important things have happened to the famous yacht since her departure to Europe two years before."[68]

Spain may have lost the war, but its monarch had gained a yacht. Refitted after the conflict, the *Giralda* became the royal yacht of King Alfonso XIII, an ardent yachtsman and racing helmsman. Colonel McCalmont, for whom the *Giralda* had been built, went on to commission an even faster yacht: *Tarantula*, one of the first steam turbine yachts built by Yarrow, the Glasgow torpedo boat concern, capable of more than twenty-three knots. *Tarantula* was launched in 1902, the year of the colonel's untimely death at forty-two, and was then purchased by Willie K. Vanderbilt, making its American debut at Newport in 1904.

The Drexels' interests, or rather Alice's, moved on as the twentieth century progressed. They would spend more time in Paris and, no doubt, aboard Tony's last floating palace, the *Sayonara*, which had been built before the Great War for a Habsburg archduke. Greatly affected by the death of his younger brother in 1934, John suffered a stroke soon after and never recovered. Alice, however, kept on spending until her demise at eighty-one in 1947. She was so frequently seen with her male secretary that when another one of Newport's grande dames, the irreverent Mamie

Fish, was asked by a Drexel relative, "Have you seen cousin Alice? I've looked everywhere in the house,"[69] Mamie is said to have replied, "Have you tried under the secretary?"[70]

Sultana, later acquired by E.H. Harriman, would also be among the American steam yachts involved in convoy duty along the Breton coast during World War I. It ended up on the west coast in the 1920s, and Hollywood would make use of the yacht for a time. Won in a raffle in 1933 by an owner who was unable to either use or sell it, the famous yacht lay neglected in a Los Angeles berth. Holed during a storm in January 1937, it sank in a channel. The Associated Press reported that the million-dollar "queen of yachts" of the 1890s was now "a battered worthless wreck."[71]

5

JULIUS FORSTMANN

(1871–1939)

Julius Forstmann, the prescient textile magnate, sensed the American economy was headed for trouble in 1927 and made a timely sale of assets to focus on building the world's largest yacht. Forstmann's wariness may well have stemmed from his own experience. In 1918, his New Jersey woolen mills were seized by the government along with other German-owned textile concerns. Although born in Germany, Forstmann was a naturalized American citizen and maintained, at the hearing that followed, that he owned $600,000 in Liberty bonds and had nothing to do with the Germans after they sank the *Lusitania*. He would later receive a Certificate of Distinguished Service from the War Department for his work in developing specifications for cloth used in Army uniforms during the First World War. Then came that day in 1926, half an hour after work began at his Passaic, New Jersey mill. With the looms whirring away at full tilt, a girl began to sing "La Marseillaise," and another, with a red flag in hand, led two thousand employees out through the gates. The long, bitter and violent strike that followed was not organized by the United Textile Workers but by a twenty-five-year-old radical, Albert Weisbord, who was a graduate of Harvard Law and a member of the Communist Party.

By 1928, Forstmann was at work on *Orion* designing the interiors of his 333-foot world traveler, which would be launched in Germany the following year. The enormous Krupp-built vessel, which displaced 3,400 tons (3,096 gross tons), was the largest yacht in this respect that had ever been built. Boasting such state-of-the-art features as electrical steering, a water filtration

Left: Julius Fortsmann, owner of the *Orion*, is pictured here in his yachting whites. *Private collection.*

Below: *Orion* underway at Newport in 1937. *The Edwin Levick Collection, The Mariners' Museum and Park, #133121.*

plant and a sonic depth finder, *Orion*'s amenities included a gymnasium, library and swimming pool. Powered by two 1,800-horsepower Krupp diesels, its maximum speed was 16½ knots. However, its cruising radius was a remarkable 23,000 miles.

Media attention followed the vessel on its maiden voyage from Hamburg to various European ports, Havana and New York, where it arrived on September 20, 1929. The *New York Times* featured a photo of *Orion* anchored off the Columbia Yacht Club's pier at West 86th Street on the Hudson and proclaimed that the palatial yacht with its crew of fifty-four was "in reality a private ocean liner."[72]

Forstmann cruised around the world, and *Orion* was in Newport in September 1937 for the America's Cup, where it would feature in one of the better Bellevue Avenue stories of the era. Invited aboard to see the first race were a group of teenage boys, Taylor and Anderson cousins, including Harry Anderson, who many years later would be the last New York Yacht Club commodore to successfully defend the America's Cup. With the contestants becalmed and the race delayed, the boys discovered a ping-pong table on *Orion*'s deck and a radio broadcasting the tennis from Forest Hill. Soon joining the fun was Ava Astor, Vincent's younger sister, who, on picking up a paddle, deposited her diamond bracelets in Harry's blazer pockets for safekeeping. The breeze eventually filled in and the ping-pong players' attention turned to the race, in which Mike Vanderbilt's *Ranger* was victorious on its way to sweeping *Endevour II*, the British challenger. Hours later, after a long day on the water, Harry dined at Rockhurst, his grandmother's Bellevue Avenue cottage, which had been inspired by a Loire Valley chateau. While serving the first course, the butler quietly inquired if he knew anything about the whereabouts of the Astor jewels. The phone had been ringing up and down the avenue, and Harry realized the fortune in stones was still in his pocket.[73]

Forstmann died in 1939, and as the gunboat USS *Vixen*, the *Orion* returned to Newport during World War II. It served as the flagship of Admiral Ernest J. King, chief of naval operations and commander of the Atlantic Fleet. After the war, as the *Argonaut*, it was a popular cruise ship, sailing the Caribbean and Mediterranean under the auspices of Raymond Whitcomb before being scrapped in Turkey in 2005.

6

HARRIETTE WARREN GOELET

(1854–1912)

On the morning of May 28, 1899, Harriette Goelet waited for her husband Robert's casket to be brought ashore from their great steam yacht *Nahma*. As if choreographed, the surreal scene was a replay of the sad day two years before when her brother-in-law Ogden's remains arrived in Newport on the maiden, transatlantic crossing of his equally magnificent steam yacht *Mayflower*. The captain's gig was made fast to the yacht club landing at the head of Sayer's Wharf, which the Goelet brothers had personally established a decade earlier. Eight sailors from the *Nahma*, acting as bearers, then carried the casket to Trinity Church, followed by the yacht's full company of seventy-two. The two brothers were interred together in the family's new mausoleum at New York's Woodlawn Cemetery. But tragedy still stalked Harriette when, three years later, her seventeen-year-old daughter, Beatrice, who was the subject of a poignant childhood portrait by John Singer Sargent, died of pneumonia.

No shrinking violet, and with her son, Robert Walton Goelet, already in his twenties, there was nothing to keep her home. Harriette turned to the sea for her solace, and perhaps it was not surprising. She had grown up surrounded by sailors. Her uncle Lloyd Phoenix, an Annapolis graduate and owner of a series of schooners, was a rear commodore of the New York Yacht Club whose magnificent Manhattan clubhouse, completed in 1901, was designed by her brother, the celebrated architect

Right: Harriette Goelet.
Author's collection.

Below: *Nahma* at the America's Cup
races in 1901. *Library of Congress*.

The USS *Octopus*, aboard which Harriette became one of the first women to take a plunge in 1911. *Author's collection.*

Whitney Warren. Harriette would have been aboard many of the yachts the Goelet brothers owned or chartered during the last decades of the nineteenth century, such as the *Norseman*, Ogden's big 132-foot schooner under the command of Newport's legendary Captain John Carley, who had taught the brothers how to sail as teenagers, and the *Beatrice*, Robert's steam yacht, which was only 56 feet overall but required a captain and crew.[74]

Given her druthers, however, Harriette would chart a different course—she would be master of her own vessel. Passing the examination for a master's certificate, she was, the *New York World* reported in 1901, "an expert in nautical affairs and quite capable of handling her own yacht in any water and in all weather,"[75] abilities recognized by the New York Yacht Club. She became one of the first yachtswomen entitled to fly the club's burgee and was also recognized by the secretary of the navy, who invited her to sail on a submarine. Boarding the USS *Octopus* at Newport in her tailor-made white serge yachting attire, Harriette became one of the first of her gender to become a submariner and actually took the helm of the craft while it ran on the surface.[76]

G.L. Watson of Glasgow, the leading British designer at the turn of the twentieth century, whose commissions had included the Prince of Wales's cutter *Britannia*, fashioned steam yachts along similar lines for the Goelet brothers in 1896. At 318 feet overall, *Mayflower* was slightly larger than *Nahma* at 306 feet, but the handsome, steel-hulled, schooner-rigged yachts replete with electric lighting and furnished by Nelson of Paris were virtually sister ships. Triple expansion steam engines could push them along at 16½ knots. Coaling could be a bit of a problem if you didn't plan ahead as the *Nahma* discovered one year in Newport when the local dealers could not supply the 380 tons required to fill its bunkers, but the steam yachts built by the Clydebank Engineering and Shipbuilding Company were as well appointed as the age could afford. Harriette, in her husband's will, received $200,000 annually and a life interest in their Fifth Avenue residence in New York and the McKim, Mead & White–designed cottage, Ochre Point, in Newport. However, she was given *Nahma* and all its fittings outright and was soon headed for blue water. Over the next decade, she would travel far and wide aboard her magnificent vessel, embarking on an itinerary that read like a Gilded Age gazetteer. *Nahma* was bound in the early years of the new century for Cannes, which Harriette thought was "about as near paradise as you can get,"[77] Monaco, Monte Carlo, Palermo, Crete, Corfu, Cartagena and Tangiers. Aboard *Nahma*, Harriette visited Athens and Constantinople in 1903, Ceylon in 1907 and the Norwegian fjords in 1910, among other ports of call. The annual regattas at Cowes on the Isle of Wight and Kiel in Germany were not to be missed. The British monarch Edward VII and the German emperor were received aboard *Nahma* on a number of occasions, but it was at Kiel week, which she attended almost every year from 1900 to 1912, that she developed her extraordinary friendship with the Kaiser Wilhelm II. A repast aboard *Nahma* with the Kaiser would be followed by an invitation to dine on the Imperial Yacht *Hohenzollern*. That the Kaiser would sit next to Harriette on some of these occasions, a matter of consequence in German court etiquette, did not go unnoticed, and he remarked in 1902 that "he had been aboard many yachts but the Nahma was the finest he had seen."[78]

At the time of Beatrice's death, the *Hohenzollern* happened to be in New York, and the Kaiser, wiring instructions from Berlin, sent its commander Rear Admiral Count von Baudisson and his aide in full uniform to call on Harriette with a message of sympathy and an extraordinary memorial—a floral wreath bound in silk ribbon with

Harriette Goelet, fifth from the left in the seated row, and her crew aboard *Nahma*. *Private collection*.

gold-edged streamers bearing the Kaiser's monogram and the imperial German crest, created by his master of entertainments.[79] Harriette, who would also be a guest at the Imperial Palace in Berlin, later endowed the Naval Hospital at Kiel.

Shipshape and Bristol fashion, *Nahma*, under Harriette's command, was a floating perfection. "I just love that ship,"[80] she allowed, and all eyes were on the beautiful steam yacht in every port of call. One crew member counted thirty photographers snapping away one morning in Cannes, a phenomenon Harriette referred to as the *Nahma* craze. The parade of visiting royals and nobles was unending, some even appearing without invitation, such as Russia's Grand Duke Michael Mickhailovich, but the yachtswoman—who did not lack in confidence—was up to the challenge. She was less sanguine, however, when the Newport navy arrived, disturbing her bliss. "Get out of my ocean,"[81] she felt like saying to fellow cottager H.A.C. Taylor when he steamed into Palermo, where *Nahma* was anchored, aboard his nearly two-hundred-foot-long *Wanderer* one spring day in 1905. The previous season she had been dismayed to see the condition of Cornelius "Neily" Vanderbilt's *North Star* looking sooty and begrimed when moored close by her own smart craft at Cannes. And although not

Kaiser Wilhelm II seen here boarding the Swedish Royal Yacht *Droitt*. *Author's collection*.

an admirer of Neily's wife, Grace, one of the "marrying Wilsons," or her sister May, who had landed an even bigger fish, Harriette's late brother-in-law Ogden Goelet, she nevertheless graciously invited the Vanderbilts to lunch, and they accepted. "During my twenty-five years [of] experience with the Wilson family, I have never heard or known of their doing a kind or courteous act,"[82] she wrote to her son the year before. Hence, we can only guess Harriette's state of mind when the next yacht arrival at Cannes proved that it could rain in paradise. It had been chartered to the Duke of Roxburghe, who had recently married May and would lay along the other side of *North Star*. Without question, it was, however, bon vivant A.J. "Tony" Drexel and his *Margarita* that most distressed Harriette. Third in the series of steam yachts Tony named for his wife, Margarita Armstrong Drexel, the immense G.L. Watson–designed floating palace was seventeen feet longer than *Nahma*. Launched in 1900, it made its Mediterranean debut the following spring. Harriette thought *Margarita* showy and fitted out in poor taste and, while she liked Mrs. Drexel, thought the jewelry-wearing Tony vulgar. During the Drexels' divorce proceedings in 1915, Tony called America "a hole not fit for a gentleman to lie in."[83]

Nahma's voyages during these years were not without incident. On entering the harbor at Venice in 1906, a pilot ran the yacht into the Italian warship *Affondatore*. Threatened with a suit, Harriette railed against the horrid pilot but paid the damages,[84] avoiding the sort of international incident that occurred three years earlier when passing the Dardanelles. Turkish fortifications fired a warning shot across the *Nahma*'s bow, mistaking the yacht for a warship since it had saluting cannons mounted fore and aft. Detained by the Turks, Harriette, having to forego a dinner engagement in Constantinople, was furious. "It is done on purpose to be disagreeable," Harriette wrote, and for "no other reason."[85] The intrepid yachtswoman demanded that the American minister seek reparation from the sultan and safe passage for the *Nahma*. After a delay of two days, his majesty proved magnanimous and the yacht was allowed to resume its passage with the Grand Cordon of the Turkish Order of Cheft bestowed on Harriette by the sultan's grand master of ceremonies on the yacht's arrival at Constantinople.

In August 1912, Harriette was reported to be suffering from cancer while aboard *Nahma* at Southampton, England, and died at her Parisian residence on Avenue d'Iena four months later at the age of fifty-eight. Her final voyage was untimely, but at least she was saved from the sea change that was about to sweep across Europe. The outbreak of the Great War

As the USS *Mayflower*, Ogden Goelet's magnificent vessel served as the Presidential Yacht from 1905 to 1929. *Author's collection.*

brought to a close the halcyon days of regattas at Cowes, Cannes and Kiel and the last vestiges of Edwardian yachting.

Nahma sailed on nevertheless, and the course of the two floating palaces built by the Goelet brothers would be astonishingly different. The *Mayflower*, acquired by the U.S. Navy in 1898, first saw service in the Spanish-American War and from 1905 to 1929 was the grand and stately Presidential Yacht. Theodore Roosevelt, the first of five presidents to have use of it, reviewed the departure of the "Great White Fleet" from the USS *Mayflower* in 1907. *Nahma*, however, would become a flagship of a different sort. After service in the U.S. Navy as a convoy escort during World War I, it came under the control of Sir Broderick C.D.A. Hartwell, a former British soldier and adventurer. As the *Istar*, it was known as the queen of the fleet along "Rum Row" off New Jersey, just beyond the three-mile limit in the 1920s. On decks where the Kaiser had been received, cases of scotch were sold to bootleggers who had eluded the Coast Guard.

On becoming federal Prohibition director for New York, Palmer Canfield, dubbed by the press as the "commanding officer of the dry fleet,"[86] decided to take a look.[87] Accompanied by newspapermen and other officials, Canfield had no trouble finding the rum fleet. "What's your cargo" he shouted to the *Istar*'s crew, who yelled back, "Lemonade."[88]

The brazen Sir Hartwell, who had his own label on the bottles he sold, sent the liquor-ladened former yacht across the Atlantic seven times. While operating off the Virginia Capes on one voyage, that captain snuck ashore near Norfolk, where, at a bank, he had no trouble exchanging $250,000 in American currency for British pounds, riding back out to the *Istar* on a ship chandler's launch.[89]

According to Erik Hofman, *Nahma* was scrapped around 1936, and its last inglorious days had been spent as a shark oil factory ship.[90]

HUNTINGTON HARTFORD

(1911–2008)

Huntington Hartford's missteps in life were legion, but Newport, where his mother bought Seaverge, the Gerry estate, in 1927, would be one of his few successes. In 1936, the young A&P heir bought the 116-foot, full-rigged ship *Joseph Conrad*, which he had found wrecked on the Brooklyn shoreline, its anchor having parted in a gale the year before. Alan Villiers, the author and mariner who had sailed the *Conrad* around the world, couldn't afford the repairs, and he sold her to Hartford for $15,000. "Hunt," as Hartford was known, spent $100,000 having it refitted as a well-appointed yacht, replete with a fireplace in the saloon.

Closely monitoring the project was Henrietta, Hunt's all-too-involved and socially ambitious mother, who became a princess after her marriage to the Neapolitan Prince Guido Pignatelli. It was probably Henrietta, Hunt's father having died when he was eleven, who was responsible for the *Conrad*'s professional crew, including Captain A.E. Toonian, who had been an officer in the Imperial Russian Navy and skipper of the *Vamarie*, an ocean racing ketch owned by Henrietta's son-in-law Vadim Makaroff.

In the summer of 1937, Hartford engaged in a highly publicized ocean race from Newport to Bermuda in which his much smaller *Conrad* was matched against the square-rigger *Seven Seas*. Built in 1912 as a Swedish training ship, the 168-foot *Seven Seas* was owned by the inventor W.S. Gubelmann and sailed by his son, Walter. The shores were thronged with onlookers, the *New York Times* reported, and there was even "a waving of handkerchiefs reminiscent of old seafaring days" as the two tall ships began the race under

Opposite, top: Huntington Hartford (*right*) and Walter S. Gubelmann aboard *Seven Seas* at Hamilton, Bermuda, following their 1937 tall ships race. *Author's collection.*

Opposite, bottom: *Seven Seas* in Newport as it gets underway for the race on August 27, 1937. *Author's collection.*

Above: Hartford's *Joseph Conrad* (dark hull) and its larger competitor, the 168-foot *Seven Seas*. *The Mariners' Museum and Park, Seven Seas, 133861.*

a "full dress of canvas."[91] After a slow passage of ten days, only one minute and forty-four seconds separated the competitors at the finish, the larger vessel crossing the line first but with the *Conrad*, winning on corrected time, given a handicap.[92]

Hunt's later adventures afloat would not be as blessed. During World War II, he served in the Coast Guard and, in 1944, was put in command of an Army supply ship, the FS-179. Bound for the Philippines with a cargo of pineapples, Hartford ran aground twice, in one instance misreading feet for fathoms. The FS ships were made famous by the 1955 movie *Mr. Roberts*, and one of Hunt's crew later recalled that Henry Fonda's and Jack Lemmon's performances in the Warner Bros. color comedy-drama were all too familiar.

The *Joseph Conrad* spent the war years as a training ship for the United States Maritime Commission. In 1947, the government gave the vessel to Mystic Seaport, where it can be seen today. Hunt would have several large motor yachts after the war that he also named *Joseph Conrad*, as he continued on his star-crossed voyages, squandering a $100 million inheritance on a kaleidoscope of failed ventures, running the gamut from a modeling agency to a handwriting analysis institute. He died at ninety-seven in 2008 at Lyford Cay in the Bahamas.

8

HOWARD HUGHES

(1905–1976)

Walter Dring never forgot his encounter with Howard Hughes one day in the summer of 1935. The billionaire had anchored his 320-foot *Southern Cross*, one of the world's largest yachts, at Brenton Cove near the narrow channel used by the steamships running into Newport. The Fall River Line's 455-foot *Commonwealth* had arrived in the wee hours of the morning from New York and narrowly missed colliding with the yacht, brushing the side of the channel bank. Suspecting damage to the hull, the superintendent of the line filed a protest with Dring, Newport's customs collector, who also received a call from the *Southern Cross*'s captain. A meeting on the yacht was arranged, at which the skipper admitted that he had moored in the wrong place and offered to move as soon as Hughes, who was ashore visiting a fellow named "Hartford," returned.[93] Appearing shortly thereafter, Hughes was anything but gracious. Offended when asked to change the anchorage for his seagoing palace, the thirty-year-old aviator charged that the real problem was that Newport "was not used to seeing yachts as big as his *Southern Cross*." Dring rattled off the list of other major yachts well known to Newport, including J.P. Morgan's *Corsair*, and Hughes moved *Southern Cross* over toward Goat Island and was gone in the morning. Hughes had traded up for the much larger *Southern Cross* from his earlier yacht, *Hilda*, in 1933, reportedly buying it in installments with European earnings from his tool company, as his estranged first wife, Ella, had placed a freeze on his assets.[94]

Southern Cross in September 1939 after it rescued some of the survivors of the *Athenia*, the first British ship sunk in World War II. *Author's collection.*

The Fall River Line's *Commonwealth* almost collided with the Hughes's yacht, which was anchored in the channel. *Courtesy of the Newport Historical Society P9216.*

Built on the Clyde by the fine Glasgow firm, Alexander Stephens & Sons, the handsome twin-screw steam yacht was considered the last word in luxury, the finest of its type built in Great Britain up to that time, other than the royal yacht. The ample deck space for entertaining, silver-toned dining saloon and staterooms replete with marble bathrooms were remarked on at the time of its launching in 1930. Hughes's embellishments included covering the huge double bed in his cabin with wolf skins.[95]

In short, it was the perfect aquatic Shangri-La for the legendary Don Juan to entertain a parade of starlets and debutantes. Among Hughes's interests during the period were Billie Dove, Ginger Rogers and Katharine Hepburn, and *Southern Cross* would be as well known to Newport as it was to Catalina. Arriving via the Panama Canal for the 1934 America's Cup races with Howard and guests aboard, the big white yacht would spend two months in Rhode Island waters.[96]

However, by 1938, Hughes had sold the yacht to Axel L. Wenner-Gren, the Swedish industrialist and Electrolux founder who was an acquaintance of Hermann Göring, the Nazi air marshal, and a suspected German sympathizer.

Howard Hughes and Ginger Rogers. *Author's collection.*

67

The bowsprit of *Southern Cross* was a bust of Elsie Mackay, the British actress and daring aviatrix who lost her life attempting to cross the Atlantic in an east–west flight in 1928. She was the daughter of Lord Inchape, the yacht's first owner. *Author's collection.*

In 1939, although *Southern Cross* was among the vessels that came to the rescue of survivors of the *Athenia*, the first British ship sunk in the opening days of World War II, some wondered if it had been providential. By 1940, the yacht was in the Bahamas, where Wenner-Gren owned Hog Island (today's Paradise Island) and was a close friend of the governor and his wife, the Duke and Duchess of Windsor. That December, the Windsors sailed to Miami on the *Southern Cross* in their first visit together to the United States, where they were serenaded by the University of Miami's band and the Duke played golf with Gene Sarazen and Sammy Snead. However, the music came to an end in 1942, when the British advised "charterers, shippers, and other interested parties not to trade with the craft."[97] The action followed the United States blacklisting of Wenner-Gren and his business interests, which included part of Bofors, the Swedish arms manufacturer in which Krupp had acquired a controlling interest between the world wars.

Elsie Mackay, whose stage name was Poppy Wyndham. *Author's collection.*

Southern Cross, Howard Hughes's love boat, was now known as the mystery ship of the Atlantic. While on a cruise to Mexico, Wenner-Gren received word of his predicament and was forced to remain there for the duration of the war. He turned his fabulous yacht over to the Mexican navy, and as the *Orizaba*, it served as a training ship. The vessel's last days are something of an enigma. It was reportedly scrapped around 1960, but, then again, there was always something mystifying about the *Southern Cross*. It was built in 1930 as the *Rover* by Lord Inchape, the chairman of the huge P&O shipping line and the father of Elsie Mackay, the stunning British actress and aviatrix whose stage name was Poppy Wyndham. The bold young woman the *New York Times* described as "steel-nerved, whether astride a horse, guiding an airplane or being 'shot' in a London studio," was determined to be the first woman to fly across the Atlantic.[98] Preparations for her 1928 flight with Captain W.R.G. Hinchliffe, a World War I flying ace, were shrouded in secrecy and unknown to her father. Attempting the difficult east–west passage during the unlikely month of March, Mackay and Hinchliffe were last seen in their single-engine plane by a ship 170 miles west of Ireland. At Long Island's Mitchell Field, five thousand waited in vain for the intrepid aviators. Eight months later, a wheel with a serial number washed ashore on the west coast of Ireland, the only piece of the plane ever found.

Lord Inchape, who was in Cairo at the time of the tragedy, would be forever haunted by his loss and sought his solace at sea. He died two years later aboard his new yacht at Monte Carlo, but Elsie was with him, as she would be with Howard Hughes and Axel Wenner-Gren—the yacht's bowsprit was a striking and unforgettable effigy of the daring and beautiful aviatrix.

9

ARTHUR CURTIS JAMES

(1867–1941)

"A silent, unassuming man who shunned publicity," is how the *New York Herald Tribune* described Arthur Curtis James in its obituary, "who, through most of his life, was better known to the public as a yachtsman than a great industrialist."[99] Yet James, the paper noted, was "a dominant figure in the control of 40,000 miles of American railroads, nearly one seventh of the nation's total rail mileage" and, at the time of his demise, was said to own more railroad stock than any other American.[100] "His crowning achievement," his biographer Roger Vaughn wrote, was the creation of "the first through passenger and freight trans-continental rail line."[101]

James was known as "Sandy" to his sailing friends, and his idea of a day well spent was at sea. Forgoing competitive sailing for the bounding main, he studied at the New York Nautical College, receiving his master's license and logging almost sixty thousand miles on his first yacht, the schooner *Cornet*, in the 1890s, including a voyage to Japan to record a total eclipse of the sun with astronomers from his alma mater, Amherst. At his side during this expedition and on the cruises that followed was his very game wife, Harriet Parsons. Together they would be bound for far-off places on their subsequent world travels on the beautiful barkentine *Aloha* (1899–1909) and majestic bark *Aloha* (II) (1910–1938.) Aboard the latter, they would circumnavigate the globe in 1921–22.

Enchanted by Hawaii, Honolulu having been a port of call on their voyage to Japan, they would bestow Hawaiian names on all their yachts. This included their two John Trumpy–designed Mathis houseboats *Lanai*

Harriet and Arthur James as they depart for a cruise around the world in September 1921. *Author's collection.*

and *Lanai* (II), built in 1912 and 1928, respectively, which served as tenders for their larger yachts, Harriet's sleek Lawley Express cruiser *Mauna Loa* and their last vessel, *Aloha Li'l*, a 126-foot motor yacht.

Clinton Crane designed the barkentine that would serve first as James's flagship when he was elected commodore of the New York Yacht Club. It was the young designer's first big commission, and with a host of construction details to keep on top of, he had not had the time to check up on the sculptor carving *Aloha*'s figurehead until just before launching. James had wanted it to be a likeness of his wife. However, as Crane later recalled when he went to take a look, he found, to his alarm, that "it had been modeled in the nude,"[102] since the sculptor assumed that's how figureheads should look. The dismayed Crane persuaded him to cover it in "Greek drapery."[103]

Among the novel features of the 160-foot steel-hulled yacht, the *Brooklyn Daily Eagle* observed, were a telescoping funnel and feathering propeller that allowed the vessel to be "converted at short notice into a square rigged ship,"[104] a capability James put to good use over the next decade crossing the Atlantic annually. Alas, what would have been a great artifact of the Gilded Age—the figurehead of Harriet—was carried away in a collision with a steamer as the yacht was bound for home in the fall of 1903.

There would be a new *Aloha* and host of other projects focusing on Newport when James became commodore of the New York Yacht Club in 1909. After renting Belvoir, the Glover villa dating from the 1890s on a hill overlooking Brenton Cove, James replaced it in 1909–10 with his Howells & Stokes–designed Beacon Hill House along with an accompanying gate lodge and extensive garage complex, a picturesque boathouse and Harriet's spectacular Blue Garden, the work of Frederick Law Olmsted Jr.

Starting in 1915, the creation of their celebrated farm group, Swiss Village, crafted by another talented designer, Grosvenor Atterbury, got underway. The difficulty of fashioning all of this from the rocky terrain of Aquidneck Island and in such a short time cannot be underestimated. Construction of the five-hundred-foot lane for Aloha's Landing, the boathouse, was formidable. It could only be accessed by a narrow right-of-way between existing waterfront estates, requiring the excavation of a trench with ten-foot rock-lined walls and the installation of a turntable at the water's end to reverse the direction of vehicles. Yet all of the undertakings were within the organizational capacity of the multitasking industrialist, and the results became a Newport must-see, delighting even Sir Thomas Lipton when he visited in 1930.

Aloha (II), which was also designed by Clinton Crane with assistance from A. Cary Smith and a great deal of planning by its owner, was in a class by herself. The 216-foot steel-hulled bark, with its separate boat deck for launches and lifeboats, crew of thirty-eight and 20,000 square feet of sail, had a rig just tall enough so it could pass under the Brooklyn Bridge. For Maud Howe Elliott, Newport's diarist, it was a "towering cloud of canvas" that brought to mind "a lovely vision of ancient days of square rigged sails and tall masts."[105] *Yachting Magazine* editor Bill Robinson called

The magnificent bark *Aloha* (**II**) underway beneath twenty thousand square feet of canvas. *Mystic Seaport Museum, Rosenfeld Collection, 1984.187.92313F.*

RESIDENCE OF E. D. MORGAN AND BOAT LANDING OF COMMODORE JAMES, NEWPORT, R. I.

Aloha's Landing, the James's boathouse and dock on Brenton Cove with E.D. Morgan's Beacon Rock visible in the background. *Author's collection.*

Aloha (II) "one of the memorable spectacles of the Era," describing a chance encounter as a kid in the 1920s, when he was bound for Nantucket on a Fall River Line steamer.[106]

As a presence when moored in Newport over the course of three decades, *Aloha* (II) became part of the capital of yachting's sense of place. The bark was an elegant ambassador for its pastime, often saluted by other craft when it arrived for the season.[107]

Below deck, the owner's quarters included a large hall and saloon and six staterooms, with the Jameses' cabin running the width of the ship. Decorative panels carved by Swedish artist Karl von Rydingsvard that are now at Mystic Seaport Museum adorned the walls, depicting the Jameses' previous vessels *Coronet* and *Aloha*, the evolution of watercraft and the Völsunga saga. So posh was the three-masted auxiliary, with amenities such as hot and cold fresh water and separate heads for every stateroom, that it became an admiral's flagship when acquired in the spring of 1917 for naval services during World War I. Rear Admiral Cameron M. Winslow, inspector of Naval Districts East Coast, held on to the beautiful armed yacht for as long as he could, and *Aloha* (II) was not returned to its owner until 1919.

An ardent advocate of his pastime, James never missed an opportunity to further yachting's interests. At Newport, he was in charge of the New

Two model boat sailors found the perfect vantage point on Goat Island in August 1930 to view this spectacle. Among the major yachts seen here are *Aloha* (II) to the right with the Ida Lewis Yacht Club off its bow and the Class J sloops *Weetamoe*, *Shamrock V* and *Resolute*. *Author's collection.*

York Yacht Club's Station No. 6 at Sayre's Wharf at the time extensive improvements were made in 1915 and acquired the Old Lime Rock Light in 1928, which became the Ida Lewis Yacht Club, James serving as its first commodore.[108]

Handling such a large yacht when in coastal waters was not without its challenges, as press accounts from the 1920s and '30s attest. Fired on in the fog east of Watch Hill by an unknown vessel while bound for Newport in 1926, *Aloha* (II) hove to for a while. Hot pursuits were not uncommon as Prohibition roiled the Ocean State's waters. Five years later, just after getting underway from Brenton Cove, the big bark collided with the mail steam ship *Sagamore* off Fort Adams. Six were injured on the steamer, which, failing to respond to *Aloha*'s horn signals, crossed its bow.[109] Then in 1934, bound for Newport off New London, *Aloha* (II) struck and almost sank the passenger ferry *Nelseco 1*, which though listing badly, was able to reach port.[110] When in port, the eternal Newport problem of uninvited guests had to be dealt with. In one such incident, an Otto Hartman from New York tried to crash a dinner dance aboard for British and American college tennis players before being nabbed, temporarily, by Newport constables, the good-natured Commodore James declining to press charges.[111]

In the mid-1930s, however, James suffered a series of heart attacks. Unable to take the physical needed to renew his master's certificate, he began to consider the future of his beloved 216-foot *Aloha* (II), aboard which he and Harriet had cruised 60,000 miles. Scuttling it, the Viking's funeral that George V had chosen for *Britannia* in 1936, was considered before the final decision was made to break it up. In October 1937, it was towed from Newport to Fall River and scrapped.

Given the press coverage that always followed *Aloha*'s sailings and landfalls, it seems odd that more media attention wasn't given to its end. The *New York Times* devoted only three sentences to James's announcement that the stately bark, which it called "one of the most famous yachts afloat," would be broken up.[112] For Newport, however, its last voyage was poignant. "She has been part of us," the *Newport Mercury* painfully observed, and the paper published a letter written by Lewis Ledoux, a resident of Newport who had seen *Aloha*'s departure.[113] "Her majestic masts seemed so rigid and bare, the absence of her yards and furled canvas made one feel peculiar and sad," Ledoux wrote as he bid farewell to the yacht, "the greatest ever afloat."[114]

SIR THOMAS J. LIPTON

(1843–1931)

Flanked by destroyers, Sir Thomas J. Lipton aboard *Erin* (II) and his challenger, *Shamrock V*, received a twenty-one-gun salute as they drew abreast of Fort Adams on their arrival at Newport for his fifth and final challenge for the America's Cup in August 1930. The cacophony of bursting shells, sirens, horns and whistles from the largest fleet of spectator craft that had ever assembled for a match built to a deafening din. At a reception that followed aboard *Erin* (II), which had moored in Brenton Cove next to Edith Bishop Taylor's *Iolanda*, Lipton received an official greeting from Mayor Mortimer A. Sullivan, Admiral Lansing of the Naval War College and Commodore Astor of the New York Yacht Club. "This is the first time I've been to Newport," the ever-gracious "Sir Tea" responded, "I've always wanted to come."[115]

For a competition so associated with Newport as the America's Cup, it's surprising the first match did not occur there until 1930, ten years after the last competition off New York. While the change in venue had been advocated by yachtsmen for years, given that sailing conditions were better on Block Island Sound, that euphemism for the Atlantic, it was actually Lipton who had long preferred New York, where his name in large red letters could easily be seen atop his eleven-story headquarters across the Hudson at Hoboken.

A walking billboard for his product, Sir Tea's jaunty image with his trademark polka-dot tie and yachting cap still grace boxes of Lipton tea nearly a century after his death. The first baronet, who had once offered to

Above: Sir Thomas Lipton aboard *Erin* (II) at Newport in 1930. *Author's collection.*

Opposite: Ned Heard, Lipton's *captain*, and the crew of *Shamrock V*, the day after their arrival in Newport, August 14, 1930. *Author's collection.*

pay Glasgow port authorities for the right to paint his name on navigational buoys, was well known to Americans, many of whom hoped he would win. Newport's diarist Maud Howe Elliott declared, "I find my own hope that Sir Thomas Lipton will win this race is generally shared."[116]

Lipton would stay aboard *Erin* (II) (ex-*Albion*) at Newport, and while the eighty-two-year-old was less visible than during the earlier challenges, rumors that he was ill were denied. He toured Newport on at least three occasions, visiting Arthur Curtis James's "Beacon Hill" and "Swiss Village." He also hosted a reception for the Rhode Island Yacht Club, met with those planning the inaugural Sir Thomas Lipton Fishing Challenge Cup scheduled for that fall, and "accepted an invitation to be the guest of Mrs. Moses Taylor aboard her yacht, *Iolanda*."[117]

There was "no one more to the fore at the Rhode Island Spa," thought the press during this era, than Edith Bishop Taylor.[118] Shortly before Moses's death in 1928, the Taylors purchased the legendary steam yacht *Iolanda*, named after the daughter of the king of Italy Victor Emmanuel III. At 318 feet overall, it was considered to be the second-largest yacht in the world at the time of its launching at Leith, Scotland, in 1908. Built for Morton F. Plant, the colorful financier and one of yachting's most capricious characters, its salons and cabins were decorated in more than half a dozen

Lipton accepted Mrs. Moses Taylor's invitation to join her aboard her 318-foot *Iolanda*, which was moored in Brenton Cove near his own *Erin* (II). *The Mariners' Museum and Park, Iolanda, P0002.001-01-154912.*

styles, and there were a laundry and hospital aboard. Unusual features were carefully reproduced when the owner sent Horace E. Boucher, a young naval architect-turned-model-maker, abroad to study and make a six-foot-long representation of the pleasure craft. The model, which can still be seen in the Model Room of the New York Yacht Club, helped establish Boucher as the Fabergé of his craft.[119]

As hostilities broke out across Europe in 1914, *Iolanda* was in harm's way, and the saga of the yacht during World War I had few equals. Placed in internment by the Germans at Trondheim, Norway, the American captain, Charles Berton, secretly chartered the *Iolanda* to the British and, under the ruse that the yacht needed repairs, sailed not for the dry docks at Bergen, as announced, but Southampton, England.

Iolanda was a charter yacht under the management of Camper & Nicholson after the war when the Taylors purchased it, and Edith, who loved the sea, remained on course with the yacht after Moses's death, living out their dream. Lipton must have been pleased to see the Gilded Age survivor in Brenton Cove, as he had lost his first *Erin*, another Scottish-built beauty, in 1915, when she was torpedoed in the Mediterranean while serving as a hospital ship.

Despite the results on the racecourse, where Mike Vanderbilt's *Enterprise* swept *Shamrock V* for races, Sir Tea appeared to enjoy his time at Newport. On the day of his departure at a luncheon aboard *Erin* for the Newport Citizens Committee and its chairman, William H. Vanderbilt, he was presented with a silver replica of the Old Stone Mill. Lipton told the committee that Newport was "a splendid place for boat racing" and hoped to race there again.[120] However, the remarkable Sir Tea, one of the Gilded Age's most interesting figures, who had risen from the slums of Glasgow to become a close friend of King Edward VII, would never return, dying in 1931.

H. EDWARD MANVILLE

(1872–1944)

Moments after Estelle Manville broke a bottle over the bow of *Hi-Esmaro*, her husband's new million-dollar yacht, a storm broke. Thousands of spectators who had gathered at Maine's Bath Iron Works on a June day in 1929 to see the beautiful flag-festooned yacht slide down the ways scattered to escape the deluge—a prelude perhaps to the threat from above the valiant vessel would face a decade and a half later at Guadalcanal and Tulagi.

H. Edward Manville, or "H.E." as he was known, took over the helm of his family's building materials business following the death of his older brother, Thomas F. Manville, in 1924. The Johns-Manville Corporation, which produced over 1,300 products, largely made of asbestos, in the 1920s and '30s, was an industrial powerhouse. (Its bankruptcy in the face of escalating asbestos litigation was still half a century away.) Edward had to move quickly, however, to establish control over the company. His brother's will, aside from having bestowed the bulk of his interest in the company to his wayward son, Tommy, also provided for a group of directors and long-term employees to acquire stock at half price.

The trouble between Thomas and his son began early, after Thomas and his wife, Valerie, divorced when Tommy was fifteen. The following year, Tommy ran away from prep school, heading west until he was finally tracked down in Boise, Idaho. At nineteen, he married Florence Huber, a Follies chorus girl he had met five days before at a matinee. His father did not attend, having thought the marriage was to take place in London, rather

At 267 feet, the beautiful *Hi-Esmaro* was said to be the third-largest diesel yacht in the world at the time of its launching with a cruising radius of twenty thousand miles and a crew of thirty-nine. *Author's collection.*

Above: H. Edward and Estelle Manville are seen here in 1929 aboard their new million-dollar yacht, *Hi-Esmaro*, with their captain on the right. *Author's collection.*

Opposite: Guests board one of *Hi-Esmaro*'s launches to see the King's Cup Race off Newport in 1934. The Manvilles loved to entertain. *Author's collection.*

than New York City Hall, so he was halfway across the Atlantic on a liner when the wedding occurred.[121]

Tommy, who would go on to set a matrimonial record, tying the knot thirteen times (his second wife was his father's stenographer), became a café society legend. Through it all, he appears to have maintained good relations with his mother, who at the time of her death in 1941 had a private veterinarian and houses within her suite at New York's swank Savoy-Plaza Hotel for each of her twenty-one dogs, mostly Pomeranians.[122]

Edward succeeded in acquiring his nephew's Johns-Manville stock as well as a sizable portion of the shares owned by company employees. By consolidating his position, he closed the door on the possibility of corporate raiders gaining control of the company. The "Asbestos Trust," as some called the concern, continued to prosper under Edward's leadership, meeting, with its diversified production lines, the expanding nation's huge need for mass-produced construction materials. In 1927, he sold control of the company to J.P. Morgan & Co., keeping a hand in company affairs as chairman of the executive committee but making time for yachting.

Hi-Esmaro, the combination derived from the first letters of the Manville children's names—Hiram Jr., Estelle, Mary and Robert—was also the name of their Westchester estate at Pleasantville, New York, and an earlier family yacht. At 267 feet, it was the third-largest diesel yacht in the world at the time of its launching. A pair of 1,200 horsepower Cooper-Bessemer engines moved it along smartly at eighteen miles per hour. With a Down East crew of thirty-nine and a cruising radius of twenty thousand miles, the Manvilles were ready to see the world, and see it they did.

When at Newport, *Hi-Esmaro* always attracted a great deal of media attention. In 1928, H.E.'s daughter Estelle married a Swedish diplomat, Count Folke Bernadotte, a descendant of Napoleon's Marshall Bernadotte and nephew of King Gustaf V of Sweden. The wedding reception at the Manville Westchester estate was attended by over 1,500 guests, and President Calvin and Grace Coolidge honored the newlyweds at a White House luncheon the following day. Awash in glamour, the young couple's presence when aboard the *Hi-Esmaro* added to the fanfare. In July 1938, brought the royal Swedish delegation, then visiting the United States, to Newport on the yacht, which was cause for celebration. The luncheons, dinners and receptions that followed, both afloat and ashore, were a high point of the resort's social season. *Hi-Esmaro* would also be a visible part of the spectator fleet at all three America's Cup defenses off Newport in the 1930s, taking such notables out to see the races as Sir Ronald Lindsay, the British ambassador; Baron Decies, the intentional polo player; Colonel Francis L.V. Hoppin, the country house architect; and Don Juan de Riano, the Spanish diplomat.[123]

In 1939, however, H.E.'s health began to fail. Acquired by the Navy in the fall of 1940, *Hi-Esmaro* was renamed the USS *Niagara* and converted to a gunboat. During the winter of 1941, it served as tender to a squadron of motor torpedo boats (PT boats) but returned to Newport that summer before sailing for Pearl Harbor. USS *Niagara*'s Hawaiian landfall occurred on October 9, but it departed on convoy duty on November 29, just eight days before the Japanese attack.

Niagara was back in Newport in 1942 to serve as a school ship for PT boats training there. New orders, however, had it underway again for the Solomon Islands before the year was out, as the fierce battle for Guadalcanal was raging.

On April 7, 1943, 177 Japanese warplanes struck the Guadalcanal-Tulagi area where the *Niagara* was tending the PT boats running security patrols. After sinking the HMNZS *Moa*, a New Zealand corvette, at Tulagi Harbor, 9

Left: As the USS *Niagara* during World War II, *Hi-Esmaro* was converted to a gunboat and served as a tender for PT boats. *The Naval History and Heritage Command photo NH82196A.*

Below: Smoke pours from the forecastle of the USS *Niagara* after being hit by a Japanese bomb as PT boats race in to rescue its crew. *National Archives photo 80-G-G8537.*

planes headed north up the Maliali River. *Niagara* and the little minesweeper USS *Rail*, moored to the riverbank, engaged the enemy aircraft as they raced toward them at no more than 150 feet above the water, a height at which the sailors could have seen the pilots' faces. The first plane crashed aflame 1,000 yards astern. Several more raiders passed through the *Niagara*'s antiaircraft fire before the fourth plane, trailing smoke, lost altitude, exploding behind hills to the north. Before the action was over, the armed yacht had bagged 6 enemy planes.

In late May, the *Niagara* was underway again, bound for New Guinea, when it was attacked by a high-flying Japanese twin-engine bomber. Taking evasive action, the helmsman swung the helm over as the bombs were released, the vessel turning just in time to narrowly miss being hit. Half an hour later, however, *Niagara*'s luck ran out when six enemy bombers appeared, dropping a pattern of bombs it could not escape. One hit the forecastle, and the sea rushed in through a hole six feet below the waterline, flooding the engine room and knocking out power. Although its main engine and steering were restored, the *Niagara* developed a serious list and was ablaze forward of the bridge as ammunition exploded on deck. With gas storage tanks at risk of blowing up, the ship was abandoned. PT boats took off the entire crew of 136. Remarkably, no one aboard was killed, and as the sailors watched, *PT-147* finished off the *Niagara* with a torpedo as flames rose three hundred feet above. The once-elegant yacht slipped below the sea.[124]

H.E. Manville died the following year. His illustrious son-in-law Count Bernadotte, in his work with the Swedish Red Cross during the war, negotiated the release of thirty-one thousand prisoners from German concentration camps and was unanimously selected to serve as the United Nations Security Council mediator for the Arab-Israeli conflict. After the war, he was assassinated by the militant Zionist group Lehi in Jerusalem, in 1948.

JESSE H. METCALF

(1860–1942)

Rhode Island's seafaring senator Jesse Houghton Metcalf, who would represent the Ocean State in the 1920s and '30s, actually went to Washington aboard his own yacht, *Felicia*. When not plying the waters of the Potomac, the U.S. senator's pleasure craft crisscrossed Narragansett Bay, escorting dignitaries to various ceremonies; leading President Taft, on board the *Mayflower*, the presidential yacht, into Rhode Island water; ferrying House Speaker Nicholas Longworth and his wife, Alice (Theodore Roosevelt's daughter), to an outing of the Republican Club of Rhode Island; and participating in yet other nautical pageants.[125]

An Ocean State native from a well-known textile manufacturing, publishing and philanthropic clan, Metcalf had two careers: serving as president of the Wanskuck Company, the woolen firm founded by his grandfather, and gradually entering public life after winning a seat on the Providence City Council in 1888. First elected to the U.S. Senate in 1925, where he would serve two terms, Metcalf was a Republican and outspoken critic of the New Deal. Concerned about rising taxes and burgeoning bureaucracy, he opposed the Social Security Act but was also fierce in his condemnation of Nazi persecution of Jews. In a 1933 Senate speech, he affirmed, "We as a nation can only declare the existence of racial or religious prejudice to be untenable as a national ideal."[126]

An experienced sailor who had won the Goelet Cup for schooners in 1887 and 1888, when he co-owned the *Sachem*, the senator was as capable as his professionals in the management of his yachts. Well known in

Jesse H. Metcalf, Rhode Island's live-aboard senator, at the wheel of *Felicia* (II) in 1930, the first of his posh yachts that went to Washington. *Author's collection.*

yachting circles, he was a member of the New York, Eastern, Larchmont and Rhode Island Yacht Clubs.

There would be three versions of *Felicia*. The first was built in 1898 for the Brooklyn inventor and munitions manufacturer E.W. Bliss and seemed to be jinxed before Metcalf acquired it in 1904. The trouble started right at its christening when Bessie Lane, a Bliss relative, failed in repeated attempts to break a bottle of wine over the bow of the 179-foot steam yacht as the hull moved away down the ways. The following year, as it attempted to land guests at the Battery in New York, *Felicia* was struck aft of the gangway by John R. Drexel's *Sultana*, carrying away its naphtha launch. Then on a July night in 1903, while under charter to Ogden Mills, the steel-hulled *Felicia*, on a passage from Newport to New York, ran up on the stern of the schooner *Druid* off Little Gull Island at the eastern end of Long Island Sound. Bound for New York from Vinalhaven, Maine, and laden with granite, the *Druid* sank in ten minutes, its captain stating that "his lights were burning and that he plainly saw the *Felicia* more than a half mile away."[127]

Under Metcalf's ownership, the yacht's misfortunes would come to an end. Yet in government service during World War I as the Newport-based USS *Felicia*, the armed yacht was again in the news, colliding with a submarine in fog off Montauk Point.

Felicia (II), the Gielow & Orr–designed ex-*Lady Betty*, which the senator acquired after the war, was 123 feet overall and gas powered. Built in 1920 by the well-regarded New York Yacht Launch & Engine Company, it was the first of Metcalf's yachts to travel to Washington and, in 1931, carried him up to the Bath Iron Works in Maine for the launching of *Felicia* (III).

A state-of-the-art, 147-foot, 10-inch, diesel-electric yacht powered by a pair of 400-horsepower Cooper-Bessemer engines, *Felicia* (III) was the first in the series to be built to the senator's specifications and was a handsome yacht attended to by a crew of seventeen.

The Washington press corps was fascinated by the lifestyle of the congressman from the Ocean State, observing that as the yachting season arrived, the senator and his wife, Louisa, would forsake their District of Columbia apartment to live aboard *Felicia*, which was moored opposite the Capitol Yacht Club. As one Ohio paper reported, Metcalf was "the lone member of Congress who has found a way to escape the South's hot nights," cruising downstream on the Potomac in the evening and returning in the morning.[128]

Up north, however, Prohibition was roiling the halcyon waters of Narragansett Bay as the Coast Guard, in hot pursuit, fired on rumrunners.

The diesel-electric *Felicia* (III), the first of the series to be built to the senator's specifications, fascinated the Washington press corps. The Ocean State's representative had found a way to beat the heat by cruising on the Potomac at night. *The Mariners' Museum and Park, Felicia, 69730.*

In July 1929, a round fired by Patrol Boat 290 chasing the motorboat *Idle Hour* at 3:00 a.m. penetrated the dining room of a house at Fogland Point, splintering furniture and lodging in the floor. The owner, W.B. Freeman, visited the senator's Providence office seeking assurances that his family would not be endangered again. Metcalf lodged a strong protest with the Coast Guard commandant, calling for an investigation. The *Idle Hour*, later apprehended at East Greenwich, Rhode Island, had no liquor aboard. Then in December, off Newport, three unarmed members of the crew of the rumrunner *Black Duck* were killed, the sole survivor stating that the Coast Guard had opened fire without warning. Seymour Lowman, assistant secretary of the treasury, called the incident "unfortunate but unavoidable."[129] In a statement issued the next day, Senator Metcalf cautioned:

> *We have national prohibition law. All our laws must be enforced. But care must be exercised in their enforcement. For years, maritime laws of the United States and other countries have provided that vessels being*

stopped on suspicion must be warned before being fired upon by a police or government boat.[130]

Prohibition became a big issue in the 1930 campaign, in which the senator was running for reelection. Before the vote, Metcalf broke with his party, calling for repeal of the dry laws.

> *It is my conviction that temperance may best be promoted, that the moral tone of the American community may be lifted to a higher plane and that respect for the law and reverence for government may be best preserved by a repeal of the Eighteenth Amendment.*[131]

His timing proved prescient, as public opinion was beginning to shift, and Ocean State voters returned the senator to office that November, although Prohibition would linger on for three more years.

Then in August 1933, just four months before the ratification of the Twenty-First Amendment repealing Prohibition, came a completely unforeseen incident linking the senator's name, once again, with the issue that had dogged him. Passing through Fishers Island Sound, not far from Newport, a handsome yacht with a smartly attired crew, flying the New York Yacht Club burgee, was stopped and boarded by the dry patrol. The commander of the Coast Guard cutter, who seized the vessel, thought it was riding awfully low in the water. His hunch proved correct when 1,600 cases of liquor were found aboard. The next morning, the press reported that the yacht in question was none other than the *Felicia* (II), which had only recently been sold by the senator.

Metcalf lost his bid for a third term in 1937 and died in 1942. His last yacht, however, the pride of the Bath Iron Works, would continue to be a familiar and reassuring sight on Narragansett Bay. As the USS *Felicia* (Pyc-35) during World War II, it sailed out of Newport on antisubmarine patrols.

13

OGDEN L. MILLS

(1884–1937)

In 1884, Odgen Livingston Mills, was born in Newport, where his family cottage Ocean Lawn stood on Bellevue Avenue. Mills was one of the most accomplished members of the summer colony between the world wars. Not content to stand behind wealth and position (his grandfather was the California financier Darius Ogden Mills), Ogden had a long career in public service. Considered an authority on government finances, he was a particularly fierce critic of the policies put into effect in the 1930s by his Hudson River neighbor Franklin Delano Roosevelt. He served in Congress, was secretary of the treasury during the Hoover administration and was even considered as a possible presidential nominee.

Acquainted with the water in Newport at an early age, young Ogden was also a sailor. Leading Harold S. "Mike" Vanderbilt in a race as a kid, he was knocked overboard when his boat jibbed as he was sailing by the lee. Catching up, Vanderbilt circled his competitor, yelling repeatedly "Do you give up?" until the furious Ogden, who was treading water and had little choice, finally gave in and was pulled aboard by the future America's Cup skipper.[132]

Ogden's affinity for steam yachts no doubt stemmed from his father's hankering for floating palaces. Although primarily a turf man, the senior Ogden Mills (1856–1939) often chartered yachts when en route to Newport from his Fifth Avenue residence in Manhattan or "Colossal" McKim, Mead and White–designed country house at Staatsburgh on the Hudson, now the centerpiece of a New York state park. Such was the case in 1911, the year Ogden's father challenged Henry Walters to a match race to Newport from

Left: Ogden and Dorothy
Mills in 1933.
Author's collection.

Below: *Surf*, the much-
chartered rent-a-yacht
and notorious rumrunner.
*Detroit Publishing Company
Collection, Library of Congress.*

the New York Yacht Club's landing on the East River. Steam yacht racing was not uncommon during the era—but not at night, hence the media's interest in the contest for a silver loving cup.

Aboard the two-hundred-foot *Surf*, a handsome steam yacht built in Scotland by Ramage & Ferguson in 1898 and brought to America by C.K.G. Billings in 1901, were a number of Mills's friends, while Sadie and Pembroke Jones joined Walters on *Narada*. Just what happened on that Friday night in September, as the great yachts raced through the night down Long Island Sound, the press could not say. It was, however, *Narada* that dropped anchor in Newport fifteen minutes ahead of its competitor. As surprising as the nocturnal race was, Mills didn't own *Surf*, although he and his son-in-law, Henry C. Phipps, often chartered it—and they were not alone. Andrew Carnegie had it in 1916 when he cruised to Nova Scotia,[133] and George Eastman, T.L. Chadbourne and Frank Graham Thompson were also known to have chartered the yacht.[134] Indeed, *Surf* appears to have been Newport's rent-a-yacht, particularly during the years it was owned by John H. Hanan, the shoe manufacturer, whose summer place, Shore Acres, was at Narragansett Pier.

By all appearances, the yacht, which had been recently sold, was on another such cruise when Lieutenants R.P. Malley and W.L. Clemmer from the USS *Cummings* were invited to board the *Surf* off Montauk Point on a June morning in 1931. A World War I destroyer that had been turned over to the Coast Guard's Rum Patrol during Prohibition, the *Cummings* had spotted the yacht at sea in the vicinity of another ship known to be involved in bootlegging and had trailed it inside the twelve-mile limit. Met at the gangway by the *Surf*'s captain in full yachting attire with gleaming gold buttons, they were introduced to a man reading a book in a deck chair who was said to be the owner. He greeted them politely but declined to let them search the yacht, as the ladies on board were feeling ill and were still in their cabins. The ruse was clever; *Surf* was not on the government's list of suspected rumrunners, and a luxurious steam yacht didn't fit the usual profile. The lieutenants, however, noticed some other irregularities on boarding that added to their suspicions. The smell of perfume pervaded, as if to mask something else. Pie plates covered some of the portholes, and the yachtsmen had dirty hands. The search that followed did not discover any women on board but did find five thousand cases of champagne and whiskey, a cargo valued at $300,000 (approximately $5,000,000 today), in one of "the most spectacular liquor captures" of the last years of Prohibition.[135]

Avalon, Ogden L. Mills's beautiful last yacht, was sold to the Canadians in 1940 and served that nation in World War II as he HCMS *Vision. Author's collection.*

While a congressman from New York in the 1920s, Mills joined the New York Yacht Club as owner of the 105-foot steam yacht *Alcalda*. Both of his wives had Rhode Island associations: his first wife, Margaret S. Rutherford, was William K. Vanderbilt's stepdaughter, while his second marriage to Dorothy Randolph Fell took place at Narragansett Pier at Wildfield Farm, the bride's father's summer place.

Avalon, Mills's last yacht, was built by the Pusey & Jones yard in Wilmington, Delaware, and launched in 1931. Designed by Cox and Stevens, the diesel-powered, 180-foot motor yacht had a distinctive and contemporary look, given its clipper bow absent a bowsprit and transom boards. The busy Mills, who at the time was undersecretary of the treasury in the Coolidge administration, serving under Andrew W. Mellon, did not wander far with *Avalon*. He appears to have used it primarily to visit his Hudson River estate and for cruises between Cold Spring Harbor near his John Russel Pope–designed country house at Woodbury on Long Island and Newport. He died at fifty-five of a heart attack in October 1937, shortly after returning from a cruise to Newport. Two thousand people attended his funeral at St. Thomas' Church in New York, including New York mayor Fiorello LaGuardia, former president Herbert Hoover and former governor of New York Al Smith, whom Ogden had run against in 1926. Among the mourners well known to the Newport summer colony were Vincent Astor, Harold S. Vanderbilt, Charles Francis Adams and the crew of the yacht *Avalon*.

14

E.D. MORGAN

(1854–1933)

Edwin Denison Morgan was a distant cousin of J. Pierpont Morgan and grandson and heir to another E.D. Morgan, the Civil War governor of New York who amassed a fortune in the securities and wholesale grocery businesses.

Known to his friends as "Alty," his grandfather having requested he change his name from Alfred Waterman Morgan after his father's untimely death in 1879, young Morgan was popular, athletic and a true sportsman. He captained the crew at Harvard and was an accomplished equestrian, the master of the Meadow Brook Hunt. Wheatley, his McKim, Mead & White–designed Long Island county house, was not only the center of his equine pursuits with an eight-hundred-foot-long stable for his many mounts but also a sports palace built around a courtyard with separate facilities for the squash courts, pool and yet other forms of recreation.

However, it was yachting that was his greatest passion, and he remained active in the pastime for more than a half century. W.P. Stephens, the yacht designer and editor, recalled that Alty "thought no more about buying a yacht than the average man does of picking up a paper as he passes a newsstand."[136] Alty's navy was so extensive that another volume would be required to chronicle it. In 1892, the *New York News* called it the largest and most costly "yachting string" in the country.[137]

No less amazing was the variety, from the catboat *Mucilage* to the America's Cup defender *Mayflower*, not to mention power yachts. He was active in the 30–40- and 66-foot classes and owned the big steel-hulled schooner

Edwin Denison Morgan.
Public domain.

Constellation and the fabled Herreshoff sloop *Gloriana*, the breakthrough design that won all eight races in which it was entered in 1891. That year, A.J. Kenealy, writing in *Outing*, hailed Morgan as a determined competitor and "one of our most zealous amateurs,"[138] qualities that no doubt led to his election as commodore of the New York Yacht Club two years later, succeeding another Newport cottager, E.T. Gerry.

Morgan's fleet of steam yachts was also extensive. Sherman Hoyt recalled in his memoirs that one of his first boat rides as a child was aboard E.D. Morgan's *Daisy*, a Herreshoff steam launch that was "a marvelous vision of shinning mahogany with brilliant brass stack and trimmings."[139]

On becoming a flag officer of the New York Yacht Club, yachting's leading consumer acquired at least six large steam yachts in the course of just six years. Included in the group was the Herreshoff flyer *Javelin*, an early commuter, and three traditional steam yachts: *Catarina* (ex–*Sands Peur*), *Ituna* and *May*.

While trading up to even larger and better-appointed steam yachts seems to have been the plan from the beginning, in one case anyway he had no choice. When Alty and *Catarina* were bound for New York from Newport in October 1890, towing the racing sloop *Moccasin* to be laid up for the winter, a nor'easter caught up with them. The posh 186-foot steam yacht, which he had acquired only the year before from the Duke of Sutherland, "encountered weather so thick they couldn't make out lights ashore, went on the rocks at Matinecock Point at 3:30 in the morning, knocking a hole into her engine room and submerging the greater part of her hull and soaking the rich and costly appointments of the interior."[140] With waves breaking over decks, Alty and his crew of thirty took to the boats and made it ashore. Meanwhile, *Moccasin*, cast off during the catastrophe with three aboard, managed to get a staysail up, the only canvas aboard. After a wild night, the sloop reached City Island at daybreak, but lacking either anchor or chain, it could only tack back and forth until a tug came to its assistance with a hawser.

While groundings of this sort usually resulted in the dismissal of the captain, Alty took responsibility for the management of his yachts. "If you

The beautiful G.L.–Watson designed *May*, E.D. Morgan's flagship while commodore of the New York Yacht Club, is seen here moored on Brenton Cove in the 1890s. *Private collection.*

wish me to engage you," he wrote to Captain W.H. Craven at the time of his employment, "it must be thoroughly understood that the boat is mine, built for my pleasure, and whatever I choose to do with her, even up to wrecking her, is only my affair."[141] *Ituna*, *Catarina*'s replacement, was only in commission for a few seasons before he sold it to buy the beautiful G.L. Watson–designed *May*, which served as his flagship while commodore. If Alty's fleet moored at Brenton Cove was an ever-changing kaleidoscope, his iconic McKim, Mead & White–designed villa, Beacon Rock, completed in 1891, was decidedly not. Perched above the cove on a rocky promontory just east of Fort Adams, this remarkable cottage with its classical colonnade is often referred to as Newport's acropolis and was actually based on the Athenian stoa of Attalos and the adjacent Agora. A yachtsman's delight with its panoramic views of the water, Beacon Rock was truly the cottage at sea. Morgan, who would hold on to the place for three decades, was quick to take advantage of the site. A turnbuckle anchored to the rock facilitated the filling of his steam yacht's water tanks by a hose run out from the house. However, the most remarkable feature of Beacon Rock was its unconventional boathouse. Lying hard against the rock in the cove on the west side was the hulk of the *Bessie Rogers*. A British bark with a cargo of pig iron, it had anchored off Goat Island in unsettled weather in August 1872 but was rammed in the fog at night by the steamer *Bristol* and quickly went to the bottom. Thereafter a hazard to navigation, it was later raised, stripped and towed over to Brenton Cove to be abandoned. Morgan was quick to see other possibilities for the wreck on acquiring the property. Noticing about six feet of water in it hold, a mean tide and that a large hole in the side left by the *Bristol* provided access, he realized he could adapt what remained of the *Bessie Rogers* as a covered boat well for his launch and tenders. Building a catwalk around the inside of the hull, quarters astern for his boatmen and a bridge to shore, Morgan's wonderful creation took form. So pleased was the yachtsman with the results that he used the boathouse, which could be illuminated at night, for entertaining, visitors making fast to a float for larger vessels on the outside of *Bessie's* hull. Nat and John Herreshoff were among the notables who docked there, steaming down from Bristol in August 1898 on the *Squib* for an America's Cup syndicate meeting with Commodore Morgan.[142]

"BEACON ROCK," ALONG OCEAN DRIVE, ESTATE OF E. D. MORGAN, NEWPORT, R. I.

Morgan's unique boathouse fashioned from the wreck of the *Bessie Rogers*. *Author's collection.*

In September 1912, a fire of unknown origin broke out aboard the old bark. Responding firemen needed help from the bluejackets at the Navy Torpedo Station at Goat Island to put out the blaze.[143] However, the damage had been done. The interior of America's most unusual boathouse had been gutted.

J.P. "JACK" MORGAN

(1867–1943)

While the Morgans would never have a marble cottage on Bellevue Avenue, *Corsair*, America's most famous steam yacht (there would actually be four), was often seen in local waters during the yachting season. Elected commodore of the New York Yacht Club in 1897, J. Pierpont Morgan (1837–1913) was followed in that office by his son J.P. "Jack" Morgan (1919–21), the member of the family Newport would see the most often; grandsons Junius S. Morgan (1933–35) and Henry S. Morgan (1946–48); and his granddaughter Jane Morgan's husband, George Nichols (1922–24). The yacht club's regattas, cruises, America's Cup defense trials and matches off Newport would be command performances for the Morgans for more than half a century. Pictures of the *Corsair* observing these contests became part of the pastime's imagery, messaging their significance and the gravitas of the yacht's afterguard.

The 241-foot *Corsair* (II), the first in the series that was actually built by J.P. Morgan, was considerably longer and better appointed than its predecessor. Designed by J. Beaver-Webb, the gifted naval architect, in 1890, it served as Morgan's flagship when commodore of the New York Yacht Club. With the outbreak of the Spanish-American War in 1898, however, Morgan's yacht was converted to a gunboat by the U.S. Navy and, as the USS *Gloucester*, drove two Spanish torpedo boats ashore at the Battle of Santiago de Cuba.

It was the third *Corsair* that Newport came to know best. Built in 1899, it passed to Jack after Pierpont's death in 1913. Jack kept the 304-foot yacht in commission until 1929, when it was given to the U.S. Coast Guard and

Opposite, top: J.P. "Jack" Morgan and his son, Junius, on the *Corsair*'s coup launch. *Mystic Seaport Museum, Rosenfeld Collection, 1984.187.784F.*

Opposite, bottom: *Rainbow* in the foreground and *Corsair* (IV) behind it during an America's Cup race off Newport in 1934. *Author's collection.*

Above: *Corsair* (III), the Morgan yacht Newport would see the most of, was built in 1899 and would be in commission until 1929. *Detroit Publishing Company Collection, Library of Congress.*

Geodetic Survey. Considered the most beautiful of all the *Corsairs*, its fine lines, the sheer of its low, black hull and absence of an elevated wheelhouse were all the work of Beaver-Webb. Its years in service to the family were not without incident, however, and the drama that unfolded on a hot July night in 1904 was both poignant and consequential for Morgan's corporate lawyer, Lewis Cass Ledyard's client relationship.

Anchored in the East River off the New York Yacht Club's landing at 24th Street—where many yachts well known to Newport were often moored during the work week—was *Rambler* (ex-*Dreamer*), a 155-foot steam yacht built in 1899 for Thomas W. Lawson, the Boston stock speculator. Having made most of his money in bear markets, he had both his private signal and the yacht's paneling festooned with the beasts. "Very few private yachts

This page: Corsair (IV) on the rocks in 1930 at Gilkey's Harbor in Penobscot Bay. *Mystic Seaport Museum 1962.1038.3.*

afloat," the *New York Times* mused at the time of its launching, would equal it in "convenience or luxury."[144] Recently acquired by Ledyard, the steam yacht had alongside its prized naphtha launch, winner of a race at Newport the year before, and considered the fastest of her type.

Light, compact and quick to generate the power needed to get underway, it's not hard to see why naphtha engines enjoyed such great popularity at the turn of the twentieth century. Making use of the hydrocarbon that appears in refining between benzene and kerosene, the naphtha engine was an 1885 invention of the clever Swedish mechanic F.W. Ofeldt. Operating on the same principle as a steam engine, the fuel was used both for vaporization in place of water inside the boilers and to fire them from below. Remarkably, they were also so new that they were exempt from the licensing and restrictions that had evolved over time governing the use of steam engines, yet the naphtha engines were just as hazardous.

At about 11:00 p.m., the watch on the steam yacht discovered that the launch, which had taken the captain ashore an hour before, was on fire. Cast off by the *Rambler*'s crew, who tried, without success, to extinguish the flames with a deck hose, the burning launch drifted toward the other steam yachts lying in the river. O.H.P. Belmont was among the revelers at a party aboard W.B. Leed's *Noma* when the guests had a close call as the wall of fire floated close by. Now fully engulfed in flames, as the fuel tank had exploded, the launch resembled the fireships used in naval warfare against anchored fleets during the age of fighting sail. On board the *Noma*, the partygoers remained on deck as they saw the launch drift toward J. Pierpont Morgan's new steam yacht, *Corsair* (III).

On board were the famous financier, his daughter Louise Pierpont Morgan Satterlee and physician Dr. James W. Monroe. The scene had now attracted the attention of all the vessels in the river and spectators ashore. The little ferry *Franklin Edson* had just cast off from 16th Street for its last run upriver to the city's infectious disease hospital on North Brother Island, where Typhoid Mary was quarantined, when its crew saw the blaze.

The month before, the *Edson* had been part of the flotilla that had come to the aid of the *General Slocum*, the big excursion steamer that had caught fire on the East River in a disaster claiming over one thousand lives, the city's greatest loss until 9/11. Making all possible speed, the ferry arrived just in time. Ledyard's flaming launch had come within one hundred feet of the *Corsair* as the ferry poured water onto the flames. The launch, which had burned to the waterline, sank.

In naval service during World War I, with Morgan's captain W.B. Porter at the helm, *Corsair* (III) was part of the small band of American steam yachts known as the "Suicide Fleet," or Breton Patrol, involved in antisubmarine convoy duty off the Brittany coast. In its first three months as an armed yacht, *Corsair* steamed 11,732 miles, true to the couplet carved in its forward deckhouse, "North, East, South and West, The Corsair sails and knows no rest." Witness to tragedies and rescuer of merchant crews, the yacht's story is told in Ralph D. Paine's *The Corsair in the War Zone*, privately printed for Jack Morgan by Houghton Mifflin in 1920.

In front of a gathering of family and friends who had arrived in Pullman cars from New York, Jane Morgan Nichols christened the palatial

J.P. "Jack" Morgan on *Corsair's* (IV) gangway on his arrival in England in 1935. *Author's collection.*

Corsair (IV) at the Bath Iron Works in April 1930. At 343 feet overall, the immense yacht, designed by Henry J. Gielow, was 10 feet longer than Julius Forstmann's *Orion* and was reported to have cost $2,500,000. Equipped with turboelectric propulsion, its 6,0000-horsepower GE diesels could move the vessel along at 17 knots. The new princess of the seas was well suited for the world voyages Morgan was contemplating and for following the contestants in the Newport debut of the America's Cup that September. However, while cruising in Maine, less than two weeks before the first race, *Corsair*'s helmsman mistook a buoy marking the channel at Gilkey's Harbor in Penobscot Bay and drove the huge yacht—the press was calling it a private ocean liner—almost half its length onto a rock ledge at high water. As the 11-foot tide began to ebb, *Corsair* listed to port with its bow thrust upward. The combined effort of the *Corsair*'s own engines and an oceangoing tug arriving from Rockland failed to dislodge the yacht, the tug's 10-inch hawser parting. "Breaking Up of New $2,500,000 Corsair Feared," bugled the *New York Times* the next morning, reporting that Junius Morgan and his wife, who were aboard at the time, had elected not to abandon ship.[145] No doubt they were reassured by the presence of their highly capable skipper, Captain Porter. At age sixteen, he had been aboard the full-rigged ship *Robert L. Belknap*, when, in 1892, it hit an unchartered rock in the South China Sea and sank. Aboard a lifeboat that capsized five times and badly lacerated from crossing coral, Porter somehow survived.

With a flood tide on the evening after the grounding, the arrival of a second tug and the Coast Guard cutter *Kickapoo*, the *Corsair* (IV) was pulled free, its double bottom credited with preventing more serious problems, and the magnificent yacht steamed on to Newport.

Junius S. Morgan, an avid small boat sailor with a penchant for designing his own yachts, including the M-Boat *Windward*, made the *Corsair* (IV) his flagship while serving as commodore of the New York Yacht Club in 1933 and '34. With the business climate not improving, Jack Morgan did not put the *Corsair* (IV) in commission in 1935, the year he sold his commuting yacht *Navette*, and the great yacht remained in dry dock at Tebo Basin in Brooklyn, under the watch of Captain Porter and a skeletal crew drawn from its usual complement of fifty-eight. It would be at the America's Cup in 1937, the year Porter retired after thirty-five years as Morgan's skipper, and Jack took four of his grandsons that year to England on the yacht, his personal physician cautioning the boys never to mention President Roosevelt's name lest it cause their grandfather to have another heart attack.[146] In 1940, *Corsair* (IV) was turned over to the British, serving in the Royal Navy during World War II. Refitted as an elegant West Coast cruise ship by Pacific Cruise Lines after the war, it would meet up with rocks that it couldn't escape off Acapulco in 1949, its salvaged power plant finding a new life providing energy for the Mexican city.

16

FREDERICK H. PRINCE

(1859–1953)

S on of a mayor of Boston, Frederick Henry Prince left Harvard during
his sophomore year. He would soon have a seat on the New York
Stock Exchange and start an enterprise that would become a meatpacking
empire comprising stockyards, slaughterhouses and rail lines. His flagship
concern, acquired in the early 1920s, was the huge Chicago-based Armour
& Company.

An avid equestrian, Fred Prince rode to the hounds, played polo and was
a founding member of the National Steeplechase Association. Princemere,
his nearly one-thousand-acre estate on Boston's North Shore, was an equine
paradise with miles of trails and carriage roads, but hardly his only horse
country holding. He also had places at polo's winter capital, Aiken, South
Carolina, and Pau, France, where he was master of the hunt. Clinton Crane,
the naval architect who got to know him well in the mid-1930s, was amazed
that this "extraordinary man" was "still riding horseback and jumping over
fences" at seventy-five.[147]

Witty, gregarious and never at a loss for words, Prince was a real character.
Reporters covering the sailing of ocean liners on the New York piers were
happy to see him as the outspoken capitalist who foresaw the 1929 stock
market crash and was always on record with his views. One scribe felt
that he had never met "a banker so entertaining."[148] Don McLennan, who

Right: Fred Prince pictured as he arrived in New York aboard the SS *Ile DeFrance* in 1938. *Author's collection.*

Below: Fred Prince (*right of life ring*) and other members of his family out for a sail on *Weetamoe* in August 1931. *Mystic Seaport Museum, Rosenfeld Collection, 1984.187.47988F.*

covered the waterfront for the *Brooklyn Daily Eagle*, learned something else about the Boston financier while investigating a story in 1935 about the SS *Manhattan*. A record number of canines sailed for Europe that August aboard the liner, including poodles, bulldogs and hounds, ten of which were owned by Prince.[149]

As a sportsman, Prince's interests extended beyond the tack room. He was a member of the Eastern Yacht Club and owned a number of racing yachts, including the Class Q sloop *Venturer* and the big 72-foot Herreshoff M Class sloop *Chiora* (ex-*Iroquois II*.)[150] Sailing through the early years of the Depression with his wherewithal intact and a gift for acquiring undervalued assets, the financier set his sights on a larger stage. In the fall of 1930, he acquired the Clinton Crane–designed America's Cup defense candidate *Weetamoe*. Built by the Herreshoff Manufacturing Company for a syndicate headed by J.P. Morgan, the 125-foot, 9-inch Class J sloop had been bested in the trials that year by Harold S. "Mike" Vanderbilt's *Enterprise*. However, it had proven itself fast in light air, and Prince, who had the accommodations improved below, took the family sailing and would hold on to *Weetamoe* until it was sold to Chandler Hovey in 1936. Palmer H. Fletcher, a young medical student who was tutor to Fred's grandson Frederick H. Prince III in the early 1930s, recalled a sail aboard *Weetamoe* when Fred decided the conditions were right to teach his wife, Abigail, how to sail. For generations who have learned how to in dinghies, even the thought is preposterous, and Fletcher remembered Prince bellowing, "Damn it, darling, you're luffing."[151] Often taking the helm during these years, Fred beat Gerard B. Lambert's *Vanatie* in several contests off Newport at the beginning of the 1932 season, but *Weetamoe* was sailed by his young friend, Mike Vanderbilt, later that summer when it won the Astor and Kings Cups. It was also that year that Prince purchased, for a trifle, the long-shuttered Marble House from Mrs. O.H.P. Belmont, Mike representing his mother in the transaction. "Well, Thomas, we've bought a house," he remarked to his manservant at the time of the $125,000 purchase, but "dammit, there is no place there for a horse."[152] Decades later, Vanderbilt reacquired it from the Prince family to present to the Preservation Society of Newport County.

For the 1934 America's Cup trials, Prince did not form a syndicate, shouldering all the expense himself. He told the press he wasn't sure what Crane's redesign of the keel and other improvements might run but that was just as well, as it might ruin his summer.[153] Crane, in his autobiography, recalled the alterations as being very expensive. Not a success, *Weetamoe*, which was sailed by Dick Boardman in the trials off Newport, was

Built in Germany in 1929, *Lone Star* is pictured here at the Harvard-Yale boat races in the 1930s. *The Mariners' Museum and Park, Lone Star, P0002.001-01-101-1245.*

eliminated, and Mike Vanderbilt's *Rainbow* was chosen over *Yankee*, which was skippered by Charles Francis Adams.

J-Class yachts require tenders, and in the 1930s, Prince had several. He acquired the 111-foot *Lawley*, built the wooden-hulled *Aide DeCamp* in 1931 and then, two years later, the considerably larger *Lone Star*, although *Starstruck* might have been a more apt handle.

Built at Kiel, Germany, in 1929 for George G. Bourne, son of the Singer sewing machine magnate, Frederick G. Bourne, *Lone Star* had the look of a Coast Guard cutter with a distinctive bald clipper bow. The diesel-powered, steel-hulled motor yacht, designed by Cox & Stevens, was certainly state-of-the-art. Palmer Fletcher thought it handsome and recalled night passages from Manhattan to Newport. Boarding with Fred's grandson in the late afternoon at the New York Yacht Club's East River landing, they would sup and sleep aboard as the *Lone Star* headed east down Long Island Sound, awakening the next morning in Newport.

Yet things never seemed to go smoothly aboard the 171-foot, 9-inch yacht. Its maiden voyage across the Atlantic was nearly its last passage.

The state-of-the-art motor yacht was powered by a pair of Krupp six-cylinder diesels. *The Mariners' Museum and Park, Lone Star, P0002.001-067-102441.*

Captain Martin Olstad told the press they "weathered seas which piled over her" and "barely succeeded in dodging two immense waterspouts."[154] He credited the yacht's cruiser build as critical to their survival. Then in August 1932, Mrs. Prince tripped over the hoisting cable for a launch as the yacht was preparing to get underway at Newport on the New York Yacht Club cruise. Falling from the bridge to the deck below, she was knocked unconscious; physicians flew in from Boston to aid in her recovery. The Newport incident involving the yacht that was truly astonishing, however, occurred in 1937. The USS *Cachalot*, first of a new class of submarines, was involved in weapons testing that summer at

The USS *Cachalot* that fired the torpedo that roiled the waters of Brenton Cove in 1937. *Author's collection.*

the Navy's Torpedo Station on Goat Island. On August 13, it fired a torpedo that veered off course, racing into Brenton Cove at twenty knots, narrowly missing *Lone Star* and Vincent Astor's *Nourmahal* as it passed between the yachts, ploughing up the lawn of Pen Craig, Hamilton Fish Webster's cottage.[155]

Prince sold the *Lone Star* to the Navy in 1941, and as the gunboat USS *Moonstone*, it was involved in antisubmarine patrols. During a training exercise off the Delaware Capes in 1943, it collided with the destroyer USS *Greer* and sank in just four minutes, with all but one aboard surviving. Lying upright in 130 feet of water near the mouth of the Indian River, it is now a popular dive site where depth charges can still be seen lined up in racks on the stern. The vessel's longest owner, Fred Prince, sailed on to his ninety-third year in 1953 and still owned, at the time of his death, the seat on the New York Stock Exchange he had bought in 1885.

17

T.O.M. SOPWITH

(1888–1989)

One of the most interesting and accomplished Newport visitors between the world wars was Thomas Octave Murdock "Tommy" Sopwith, the British aviation pioneer and airplane manufacturer who challenged for the America's Cup in 1934 and '37.

His Sopwith Camel, the World War I single-seat biplane, introduced in 1917, was the most successful Allied fighter on the western front. Credited with downing over 1,200 enemy aircraft, Sopwith Camels were often engaged in aerial combat with Fokkers, the German fighters developed by the brilliant Anthony Fokker (1890–1939). A Dutchman sent to Germany by his father to become an automobile mechanic in 1910, Fokker became so consumed by his interest in aviation that he opened his own aircraft factory in Berlin two years later. Manfred Von Richthofen, the German ace with eighty air victories, famously known as the Red Baron, flew a Fokker Dr-1 Triplane.

When, during the lead up to World War II, the British government failed to comprehend the threat posed by Hitler's rearming, it was Sopwith who, again, played a huge part, tooling up his factories to produce one thousand airframes without having received a single order from his vacillating government—forethought that helped the Royal Air Force defeat the Germans three years later in the Battle of Britain.

A sportsman extraordinaire, Tommy's myriad interests ran the gamut from ballooning to ice hockey, where he was a member of the British team that won the European Championship in 1910.

T.O.M. Sopwith and his wife, Phyllis, his timekeeper in both his America's Cup challenges, pictured in 1937. *Author's collection.*

His interest in yachting was lifelong. A fishing cutter acquired in 1907 was the first of some sixteen motor and sailing yachts, including four twelve-meters and three J-Class racing yachts. Laurels afloat among his more than one hundred presentation pieces included the 1912 Harmsworth, the British International Trophy won at the helm of the speedboat *Maple Leaf IV*, and

Right: Anthony Fokker.
Author's collection.

Opposite: *Endevour* tuning
up with *Endevour* (II) in the
background off Newport
on August 15, 1937.
Author's collection.

three Twelve-Meter championships. With his company prospering between
the wars, Tommy became enamored of ever-larger motor yachts. There
would be five, the last two serving as tenders while at Newport to J-Class
challengers *Endeavour* and *Endeavour II*. *Vita III*, which had the duty in 1934,
was a 742-ton beauty, the ex-*Argosy*, designed by Cox and Stevens for Charles
A. Stone, father of the commodore on whose watch the New York Yacht
Club would finally lose the America's Cup in 1983. She was replaced in 1937
by the 1,600-ton, 263-foot *Philante*, a state-of-the-art, handsomely appointed
world traveler that was even designed with special storage compartments for
sails and tackle from Sopwith's racing yachts. *Philante*'s name was derived
from the combination of that of his wife, Phyllis, and son, Thomas Edward.

So much has been written over the years about Sopwith's 1934 and '37
America's Cup challenges that there is no need to cover this ground again.
Suffice it to say that he had no chance in 1937 against the super J-Class
sloop *Ranger*, the state-of-the-art Starling Burgess and Olin Stephens design
developed through tank testing that swept *Endeavour II* in four races. However,
in 1934, Tommy almost succeeded in wresting the cup away. Leading two

races to none, he was ahead in the third when his despairing competitor, Mike Vanderbilt, turned over the helm to Sherman Hoyt and went below. The wily old Hoyt then fashioned the most improbable of comebacks. Keeping high of the course to the finish, he fooled Sopwith into unnecessary covering tacks, sailing through *Endeavour II*'s lee when it tacked back toward the line. The New York Yacht Club's Race Committee refusal to hear a Sopwith protest after the next race, because he had not flown the required

Endevour followed by T.O.M. Sopwith's tender *Vita* III (ex-*Argosy*) off Bristol, Rhode Island, on August 15, 1934. *Author's collection.*

flag at the time of the incident, long rankled as the Americans came back to win the match in six races. It was after the fourth race sailing back to Newport with his crew and wife, Phyllis, who served as his timekeeper, that an extraordinary thing happened. Sopwith remembered he was very tired when a launch pulled up alongside *Endeavor II*, and a tall fellow at the helm said, "You Sopwith?"[156] Tommy replied in the affirmative, and the stranger replied, "I'm Fokker."[157] The two legends of early aviation, who had never met, stared at each other across a patch of Narragansett Bay as Sopwith exclaimed, "Christ! Come on board and have a drink."[158]

Both would be back in Newport in the late '30s, Sopwith for his second challenge three years later and Fokker, who had moved to the United States in the 1920s, with his new motor yacht *Q.E.D.* in 1938. Launched that June at the Harlem River yard of the Consolidated Ship Building Corporation, the 110-foot, streamlined eye-catcher looked like something Raymond Loewy would have created, but was actually Fokker's attempt to apply aircraft technology to yacht design. Lightly constructed with a

Q.E.D., Fokker's attempt to apply aircraft technology to boatbuilding, was the work of yacht designer William Atkin. *The Mariners' Museum and Park, Q.,E.D, 137946.*

plywood superstructure, the *Q.E.D.* must have been pretty damn quick, with a power plant consisting of an 800-horsepower Vinalert flanked by a pair of 500-horsepower Wright-Typhoon engines driving triple screws. Fokker, who had also designed the craft's stabilizer, announced, at the launching, that his novel yacht would "revolutionize the shipbuilding industry."[159] He also hoped, in the interest of progress, that the *Q.E.D.* would be "obsolete within two years," as there were "too many yachts which outlived their owners."[160] Fokker's wish was fulfilled in October 1939 when the *Q.E.D.* caught fire and sank in the Hudson River off Yonkers. Two months later, he was gone as well, of meningitis, at forty-nine.

Knighted in 1953, Sir Thomas continued his remarkable career in aviation after World War II. The pioneer's 100th birthday in 1988 was celebrated with a flyover of his Hampshire estate by many of the fighter planes he had developed over the better part of a century. *Philante* served as an armed yacht in the Royal Navy during World War II, and since 1947, it has been the Norwegian Royal Yacht *Norge*.

CORNELIUS "NEILY" VANDERBILT

(1873–1942)

Pictured here on the bridge of his steam yacht *North Star* in full yachting regalia, Cornelius "Neily" Vanderbilt III was the personification of the Gilded Age commodore. He was a stickler for proper "yachting routine," the pastime's extensive etiquette; Vanderbilt's son would later recall the boarding ritual his father always observed. At the dock when boarding *North Star*'s steam launch, the boatswain held the boat hook while one sailor tended the engine and two stood at attention saluting Vanderbilt, who would always be the first to step aboard. Donning his yachting cap only while afloat, he would again be saluted by Captain Timpson and the yacht's crew on boarding his steam yacht. As commodore of the New York Yacht Club in the twentieth century's first decade, he helped foster international yachting relations and was received by a galaxy of old-world nobility, including the German emperor Kaiser Wilhelm II, Czar Nicholas II of Russia and the United Kingdom's monarchs King Edward VII and his son George V. On their visits to America, he in return would host Prince Henry of Germany, Duke Boris of Russia and, after World War I, King Albert and Queen Elizabeth of Belgium. Nor did Vanderbilt ever seem to relinquish his role as the pastime's ambassador, welcoming aboard his motor yacht *Winchester* in the 1930s to see the America's Cup matches such foreign dignitaries as the British ambassador, Ronald Lindsay.[161]

The red carpet was not extended to all in high places, however, such as at the Harvard-Yale boat races on the Thames River near New London one year. A tide change brought together, unexpectedly, the sterns of *Winchester*

Left: Cornelius "Neily" Vanderbilt III, seen here aboard the North Star. *Mystic Seaport Museum, Rosenfeld Collection, James Burton photographer, B.1984.187.457.*

Below: *North Star*, Neily's 256-foot flagship when commodore of the New York Yacht Club, had three previous owners and was converted for use as a British hospital ship during the Great War. *Detroit Publishing Company Collection, Library of Congress.*

and Vincent Astor's *Nourmahal* with President Franklin Delano Roosevelt aboard. FDR waved and asked the Vanderbilts to join them, which the commodore declined to do, noting that it was yachting practice that such an invitation could only be extended by the owner. The president laughed, saying he waived "all those customs," at which point, Mrs. Vanderbilt rose from her deck chair, moved toward the rail and said, "I don't like you, Mr. President," and then doubled down, "I don't like you at all."[162] FDR replied genially, "Well, Mrs. Vanderbilt, lots of people don't like me, you're in good company."[163]

Vincent Astor then appeared at the rail to extend the required owner's invitation, and the Vanderbilts did visit. FDR, exercising his famous charm, even seemed to have made some progress with Grace Vanderbilt, who, on departing, declared that while she wouldn't vote for him, she wouldn't vote against him.

Educated at Yale's Sheffield Scientific School, "Neily," as he was known to his friends, earned a degree in engineering and was keenly interested in the mechanical aspects of his family's railroad empire. He went on to patent more than thirty inventions for improving locomotives, tanks and freight cars. His interest in transportation also extended to subways, which he had studied abroad, and he worked with August Belmont to establish New York's first line, the I.R.T.

Joining the New York State National Guard in 1901, Vanderbilt also had a long and distinguished military career. He served in the Punitive Expedition against the Mexican revolutionary Poncho Villa in 1916 and overseas with the American Expeditionary Forces on the western front during World War I as commander of the 102nd Engineers. He rose to the rank of brigadier general, and his many decorations included the Belgian Croix de Guerre. Yet for all his attainments, Neily's life would forever be defined by one of the great injustices of the age: he was famously disowned by his disapproving parents for marrying a beautiful southern belle, Grace Wilson, in 1896. When his father died three years later, he received only $500,000 and interest from a million-dollar trust fund, rather than the greater part of an estate valued at $70 million. The bulk of the fortune passed to his younger brother, Alfred, who gave him $6 million, but Neily would never have the wherewithal—that prerequisite for yachting on a grand scale—of his cousins and fellow yachtsmen, "Willie K." and Harold "Mike" Vanderbilt. As the years went by, this would become increasingly apparent.

On Bellevue Avenue, Neily and Grace would first rent and then buy, in 1911, Beaulieu, the mid-century cottage of the William Waldorf Astors,

Grace Wilson Vanderbilt with her back to the camera and her sister, May Wilson Goelet, holding a parasol aboard the *North Star* in 1903. *The Preservation Society of Newport County.*

who had moved abroad. They would race together aboard Neily's Newport Seventy *Rainbow*, the *Brooklyn Daily Eagle* observing that it was "one of the peculiarities of the races of the seventy-footers that every time *Rainbow* has won, Mrs. Vanderbilt has been aboard."[164] Grace's in-laws, however, considered her anything but heaven-sent. Two years older than Neily, it was rumored that her previous engagement to Cecil Baring, Lord Revelstoke's son, had been broken by her for reasons of financial insufficiency. In the eyes of Cornelius and Alice Vanderbilt, Grace was a seasoned fortune hunter and her family was also thought circumspect. One of the "marrying Wilsons," her sister Belle married Sir Michael Henry Herbert, the younger

brother of the Earl of Pembroke, while sister May was Mrs. Ogden Goelet. Also suspect, in the eyes of the Vanderbilts, was her father, Richard T. Wilson, a Confederate commissary general turned New York investment banker, who was an alleged war profiteer.

At thirty-four in 1907, Vanderbilt would acquire the latest Herreshoff creation, a one-design "57-footer," twice winning the Astor Cup for sloops with *Aurora*. His racing career appears to have concluded, however, even before he departed for France.

After the war, he owned a series of legendary yachts, starting with Morton F. Plant's beautiful schooner *Elena* in 1918, after the financier's death, and in 1922, the 1905 Transatlantic Race winner, *Atlantic*. Nevertheless, while his cousins were building their fabulous sailing and motor yachts, the general was relegated to vessels already in their declining years. He was the fourth owner of *North Star*, which he kept abroad for economy, and it was at Cowes when the Great War broke out, finding use during the hostilities as a hospital ship for the British Red Cross. The *Atlantic*, which was almost lost in a fire at Marseilles in 1923, he had for only four seasons. *Winchester* (IV), the 225-foot steamer he owned in the 1930s, and the *Atlantic* both had three previous owners, not to mention naval service during World War I. Shortly after Vanderbilt acquired *Winchester* (IV) from the estate of Russell A. Alger, a gas tank exploded while the craft was anchored off the New York Yacht Club's East River landing, rattling Manhattan windows and

Opposite: *Winchester* (**IV**), the aging 225-foot steam flyer Vanderbilt owned in the 1930s. *Author's collection.*

Above: Captain J.F. Carter (*left*), Grace Vanderbilt and her father, Cornelius "Neily" Vanderbilt, aboard the *Atlantic* in October 1925. *Author's collection.*

sending a plume of smoke and flames aloft that was observed as far away as the Chrysler and Chanin towers. Extensive damage resulted, and a good portion of *Winchester*'s inaugural season with the general was spent being overhauled at the Todd shipyard.[165]

Built in 1916, the battleship gray flyer, which resembled a destroyer, was fast but known as a wet boat, and with a beam of just twenty-one feet, it rolled in a seaway. The aging vessel was a far cry from the marvelous diesel-powered motor yachts his cousins were building at the time. Willie K. Vanderbilt's *Alva* had a beam of forty-six feet, and the world traveler was awash in amenities.

As the 1930s progressed, with his assets further diminished by the collapse of the stock market, the general was challenged even to put *Winchester* in commission. According to his son, it cost $7,000 a month "just to keep the *Winchester* tied up at the dock and at least twice that much on long cruises."[166] Neily's sisters, Gertrude Vanderbilt Whitney and Gladys, Countess Szechenyi, helped, as did his mother, Alice Vanderbilt, writing at the start of one season:

> *Dear Neily, I would like to give you a present for the summer and it would be such a pleasure to me if you will put the Winchester in commission for three months. I know you enjoy her and want you so much to have her this summer. Love, Affly Yrs, Mother*[167]

A bequest from Alice's estate at the time of her demise in 1934 helped the general avoid insolvency. Yet Grace, who had become a leader of New York and Newport society, continued to entertain lavishly. Eschewing the social scene, Neily became reclusive, living aboard *Winchester* (IV) at the Miami Boat Basin, a venue that was a far cry from Willie K.'s winter Shangri-La, Alva Base on nearby Fisher Island, replete with everything from a pier for his 264-foot private ocean liner to a seaplane hangar and golf course with holes named for his yachts.

Depressed about his finances, concerned about Grace's extravagances and alienated from many in his family, the general's last years were not pretty. In 1940, he sold *Winchester*, which, as the HMCS *Renard*, served in the Canadian Navy during World War II. In declining health thereafter, he continued to live at the basin in a chartered houseboat, dying of a brain hemorrhage in 1942 at sixty-eight.

Unlike many Vanderbilt unions, however, Grace and Neily never divorced. On a train headed south during his last illness, she had reached

Grace and Neily Vanderbilt at Newport in 1933. *Author's collection.*

Jacksonville when word was received of his death. Accompanying the general's coffin back to New York with a military honor guard, she returned to their Fifth Avenue residence, secluding herself in his study for long periods and then, on the night of his funeral, locked the door and never entered the room again.

FREDERICK W. VANDERBILT

(1856–1938)

Frederick W. Vanderbilt, who built and owned Rough Point (1887–89) and summered there for several decades, was the saltiest of William H. Vanderbilt's children and the grandson of the fortune founder, Cornelius Vanderbilt. Secretly marrying at twenty-two a divorcée twelve years his senior, Louise Anthony Torrence, Fred experienced early the displeasure of his family. Left only a fraction of what his brothers, Cornelius and William, received from their father's estate, he nevertheless prospered. Learning the railroad business in the offices of his family's New York Central Railroad, the unassuming and astute young man became a successful executive, serving, eventually, as a director of twenty-two railroads and amassing a considerable fortune.

Owner of many yachts well known to Newport, Fred took President Chester A. Arthur for a sail during Arthur's visit to the "City by the Sea" in 1883 aboard his schooner *Tidal Wave* and later had the steam yachts *Vedette* (I–II), *Conqueror* and *Warrior*. By far the largest was the magnificent 282-foot *Warrior*, considered to be one of the best designs of the great Scottish naval architect, G.L. Watson, whose Gilded Age client list included Sir Thomas Lipton and the Prince of Wales. At Troon, Scotland, in 1904, Vanderbilt boarded the yacht for its maiden voyage to Havre, where its opulent interiors were installed by "a firm of Parisian upholsterers and decorators."[168] Carved Spanish walnut graced the dining saloon, executed in the Louis XV style, while the Louis XIV motif graced the drawing room and the owner's cabin. Vanderbilt traveled far and wide aboard *Warrior* with its crew of forty and long-serving Scottish captain, W.L. McLean, until an ill-starred winter cruise in 1914. Bound for Cuba and points south, it ran aground in rough water near the mouth of Colombia's

Magdalena River with not only her owner aboard but also Mrs. Vanderbilt, Lord Falconer and the Duke and Duchess of Manchester.

Alerted by wireless, the United Fruit Company's steamer *Frutera* and other vessels rushed to the rescue. Eight of the *Frutera*'s lifeboats were smashed and another capsized in the opening hours of the effort and, with waves breaking over the yacht, it wasn't until the seas had moderated that the owner's party was finally taken off. Despite the peril, Captain McLean and his crew remained aboard as the made-for-media drama played out for months in the press.

Frederick W. Vanderbilt.
Roosevelt-Vanderbilt National Historic Site.

Miraculously refloated that spring, *Warrior* was towed to New York by a wrecker, where it was overhauled at Staten Island. However, when the *Warrior* returned to Newport that summer, Vanderbilt was no longer at the helm. "Mr. Vanderbilt, who has long been one of our foremost yachtsmen," the *Pawtucket Times* reported, "has given up yachting entirely."[169] Harry Payne Whitney, who was married to Fred's niece,[170] was the new owner, and the now famous yacht would sail on for years until, as the HMS *Warrior*, the Luftwaffe caught up with it in the English Channel in 1940.

Two years ashore proved transformative nevertheless, and in 1916, Vanderbilt purchased the *Virginia*, another G.L. Watson design, built in 1899 by the Bath Iron Works. The 199-foot, 6-inch steam yacht was renamed *Vedette* (II), the name he had given his first steamer in the 1880s. As the USS *Vedette* during the Great War, it was part of the famed Breton Patrol of American armed yachts engaged in convoy escort duty off the French coast. *Vedette* was returned to Vanderbilt in 1919, but by 1924, the year he and Louise, tiring of the Newport scene, bought their Bar Harbor villa, Sonogee, he would have a new 158-foot, 6-inch *Vedette* (III). Designed by Irving Cox of Cox & Stevens, the handsome diesel-powered yacht was built in Denmark by Burmeister & Wain. Estimates as to the yacht's cost varied. The *New York Times* thought $450,000 with the furnishings from "Parisian art rooms" and other features bringing it to $1 million.[171] Indeed, the Vanderbilts' affinity for French decorative arts—as evidenced by their previous yachts and Hudson River estate Hyde Park, where some of the furnishings had come from Napoleon Bonaparte's Malmaison Palace—was well demonstrated. Just how *Vedette* (III) interiors fared the following January, when the vessel sank in a

Brooklyn boat basin, can only be imagined, but Fred, who had his share of "that's yachting" disappointments, soon had it in commission again.

In 1926, however, Vanderbilt lost his partner in life when Louise died suddenly in Paris. He would be in Newport aboard *Vedette* (III) the following summer, spending a night at Wakehurst, the cottage of his niece by marriage Margaret Louise "Daisy" Van Alen, but his last years were to be reclusive and spent at Hyde Park, where he died in 1938. Fred not having any offspring, his yacht and much of his estate were inherited by Daisy. Sold in 1939, *Vedette* (III) began a new chapter as the pilot boat *Baltimore*, and after being requisitioned by the U.S. Navy in 1941, it continued to guide ships as the **USS YAG-7**.

WILLIAM K. VANDERBILT II AND HAROLD S. "MIKE" VANDERBILT

Williama K. Vanderbilt II (1878–1944), known as "Willie K." or just "Willie," and his younger brother, Harold S. Vanderbilt (1884–1970), "Mike" to his friends, would be among the best known and most accomplished yachtsmen of their generation. Great-grandsons of the fortune founder, Cornelius Vanderbilt, they were also examples of the phenomenon that Kenneth T. Jackson has noted was part of the American experience for, "as leisure time increased, compulsive play became an accepted alternative to compulsive work."[172]

Although their father, William K. Vanderbilt (1849–1920,) who had built Marble House on Bellevue Avenue for their mother, Alva, was primarily a turf man, the fortune he had inherited on his father's death in 1885 gave "full vent," as his daughter Consuelo put it, to her mother's ambitions. "The yacht *Alva*, of 1400 tons," Consuelo recalled in her memoir, was "one of the first results of our new affluence."[173]

The *New York Herald* did not know what to make of Vanderbilt's huge 285-foot steel-hulled world traveler:

> *The barkentine rigged* Alva *of W.K. Vanderbilt does not look like a yacht but resembles far more a transatlantic liner. She is not as graceful as the*

Opposite, top: *Warrior*, Vanderbilt's beautiful G.L. Watson–designed, 282-foot steam yacht, was almost lost off the coast of Colombia on a winter cruise in 1914. *Library of Congress.*
Opposite, bottom: *Vedette* (III), last in the long line of Fred Vanderbilt's yachts, was built in Denmark in 1924 and, as seen here, later served the nation as the pilot boat USS YAG-7 during World War II. *National Archives and Record Administration, 19-N-YAG7-87160.*

Valiant. Library of Congress.

other yachts but her appearance is overpowering among the dainty and delicate craft which form the fleet.[174]

Alva also proved to be a bad sea boat and, just a half-dozen years after its launching, while bound from Bar Harbor to Newport, went to the bottom after being rammed in the fog off Cape Cod's Monomoy Point in 1892. Its replacement, *Valiant*, completed the following year, was the largest based on Thames tonnage and one of the most opulent floating palaces of the Gilded Age. Just how to portray this embodiment of American excess seems to have been a problem for the great maritime artist of the era, Edoardo De Martino, "Marine Painter in the Ordinary" to both Queen Victoria and Edward VIII, who, in his near tryptic of a regatta off Cannes in 1895, depicted the enormous steam yacht bow on, rather than have it overwhelm his panorama of the fleet. Vanderbilt held on to *Valiant* until 1910, long after Alva had jumped ship to marry her husband's best friend and frequent cruise companion, O.H.P. Belmont, whom she had fallen for while bound for India on the yacht in 1893.

Willie K. and his first wife, Virginia Graham "Birdie" Fair, who excelled at outdoor sports. *Courtesy Suffolk County Vanderbilt Museum.*

Consuelo recalled she and her brothers found the yachting expeditions on the steam yachts with their tutors aboard boring as children, yet it is likely that they kindled in the boys their later affinity for the sea.

Never a student, Willie K.'s path would be different. He left Harvard after his sophomore year, no doubt a matter of mutual relief with the faculty, to marry Virginia Graham "Birdie" Fair in 1899. A vivacious young woman who excelled at outdoor sports, she was the younger sister of "Tessie" Oelrichs, who, with her husband, Hermann, was then building their Bellevue Avenue villa, Rosecliff. One of the great Gilded Age Newport romances, Birdie and Willie K. seemed perfectly matched and inseparable. She would be with him on land and sea and was just as capable at taking the wheel or helm as the young couple tore through the century's first decade.

Dustups with Newport's constables, who enforced the speed limit for "motors," as early automobiles were often called, at ten miles per hour, were inevitable and well documented by the press. "Arrest me every day if you want to," Willie K. is reported to have said. "It is nothing to pay fines for such sport."[175] On another occasion, he complained that automobiles in the City by the Sea could not "raise dust in the streets without someone complaining."[176] Willie K's. sister, Consuelo, had seen a measure of "reckless daring"[177] in her brother as a child, but Clinton Crane, his friend and naval architect, who had driven with him, noted that while Willie loved to go fast, he was an excellent driver.

He would soon find the climate more hospitable for motors elsewhere, setting the world land speed record in France in 1902; organizing the nation's first major auto racing competition, the Vanderbilt Cup races, on Long Island two years later; and building the first limited access highway, the Long Island Motor Parkway, in 1908.

Newport's "oldest boatman," Captain Tim Shea, well known to the cottagers, taught Willie K. how to sail.[178] His first yacht, the *Osprey*, was a Herreshoff half-rater that he raced off Newport as a teenager and was followed by the *Carmita*, a 45-foot sloop, aboard which he and Birdie explored Narragansett Bay. However, in 1900, he joined other well-heeled yachtsmen to build the Newport "Seventies," the first one-design class of larger racing yachts. Although 70 feet on the waterline, the big Herreshoff sloops were 106 feet overall, and Willie K., who named his *Virginia* for Birdie, competed against his cousin Cornelius's *Rainbow*, August Belmont's *Mineola* and *Yankee*, which was jointly owned by Harry Payne Whitney and H.B. Duryea. While his cousin and August Belmont hired professional captains for their "Seventies," Willie K., a devoted amateur, or Corinthian, was determined to steer his own boat. This led to some trouble with his Scandinavian crew, who complained after losing some races that the yacht had been badly handled by Vanderbilt. As the first season progressed, their skipper steadily improved. In 1901, he won a series off Newport, and a few seasons later, Vanderbilt, who was then commodore of that hotbed of amateur sentiment, the Seawanhaka Corinthian Yacht Club, organized a completely nonprofessional crew for the *Virginia* with Clinton Crane.[179] Yet as Crane recalled in his memoirs, Willie "was always more interested in power boats."[180]

In 1904, he acquired the *Tarantula*, a state-of-the-art, turbine-powered steam yacht that had been built by Yarrow, the famous British torpedo boat and destroyer yard. Steam yacht racing was then coming into vogue, and Vanderbilt retained Crane to increase the speed of the bodacious 153.5-foot flyer, which had more the look of a warship. A challenge made to Charles R. Flint, whose C.D. Mosher–designed *Arrow* had set the world speed record on water in 1902, was not accepted. *Tarantula* did compete, however, in some exciting and much publicized match races against Howard Gould's *Niagara*

Tarantula, Willie K.'s state-of-the-art turbine-powered steam yacht, seen here in New York's East River. *Photographed by Nathaniel Livermore Stebbins, June 20, 1907, Historic New England.*

Top: With nine propellers on three shafts, *Tarantula*'s huge wake soon caused Willie K. problems. *Author's collection*.

Bottom: Rosamond Lancaster Warburton became Willie K.'s second wife in 1927. *The Mariners' Museum and Park, Vanderbilts, 112275*.

IV along Long Island's North Shore, winning one and losing another. The big new boilers Crane installed to increase speed turned nine propellers on three shafts. Unfortunately, when Willie used the steamer to commute to Manhattan via the East River, it threw up a wake that, Crane recalled, "broke like surf on the shore,"[181] washing over docks and piers. Damage claims poured in, and Vanderbilt lost at least one court case. Willie's lawyer sought Crane's assistance in keeping his client off the river. Thereafter, Willie seems to have used *Tarantula* when bound for Newport and as a tender for the *Virginia* and his small race boats, *Mercedes VI* and *Hard Boiled Egg*, the last so-named because it could not be beat. To the delight of the press, Birdie was at the wheel of *Hard Boiled Egg* as it crossed the line to win a race off New Rochelle, but the young couple were soon to part, separating in 1910 over a number of issues, not the least of which was the young yachtsman's affair with Parisian actress Mademoiselle Polaris.

Willie K.'s visits to Newport were less frequent thereafter. In 1922, he built a marine museum at Eagle's Nest, his waterfront estate at Centerport on Long Island's North Shore, and acquired *Ara*, a 213-foot French warship that had been re-fitted as a yacht, and began his well-chronicled oceanographic voyages in search of marine specimens.

However, he was in Newport in September 1927 aboard *Ara* with his new bride, Rosamond Lancaster Warburton. They had married the month before in Paris, and Willie gave a luncheon on board as the couple visited friends in the summer colony. It was also from the Rhode Island port in 1931 that Vanderbilt, who had received his mariner's master's certificate in 1918, began his circumnavigation of the globe aboard his last great yacht *Alva* (II), and was again there for the 1934 America's Cup with the 264-foot, palatial voyager, this time with a twin-engine seaplane perched dramatically on its stern.

Built by Krupp in Germany in 1930 and designed by Cox & Stevens, the premier firm also responsible for *Nourmahal* and *Sea Cloud*, this diesel-powered *Alva* (II) boasted, among its many amenities, interiors that resembled a posh Fifth Avenue apartment, a fully equipped gymnasium and a laboratory for scientific work. Alva's Base, the yacht's winter home at Fisher's Island in Florida, was replete with pier, seaplane hangar, golf course, swimming pool, tennis courts and residence designed by Maurice Fatio. Yet the halcyon days would last for only a decade, and with war imminent, Vanderbilt gave *Alva* to the U.S. Navy a month before Pearl Harbor. His sister, Consuelo, felt, in doing so, he knew in his heart that he would never go to sea again on his beloved yacht. As the USS *Plymouth*, after having been converted to a patrol gunboat,

Alva (II), Willie K's 264-foot diesel-powered world traveler, was built by Krupp in Germany in 1930. *The Mariners' Museum and Park, Alva 112269.*

Alva's saloon had the look of a Park Avenue living room. *The Mariners' Museum and Park, Alva 112246.*

An elegantly appointed marble head aboard *Alva* (II). *The Mariners' Museum and Park, Alva 112248.*

Willie K. gave *Alva* to the Navy just before Pearl Harbor. Converted to the patrol gunboat USS *Plymouth*, it would be sunk by a German submarine while on convoy duty off Cape Henry, Virginia, in 1943 with the loss of almost half the crew. *Suffolk County Vanderbilt Museum.*

Willie K.'s pride and joy would be sunk by a German submarine while on convoy duty off Cape Henry, Virginia, in August 1943. Only 85 of the crew of 155 officers and men survived. The armed yacht sank within two minutes, and rescue efforts were stymied by heavy seas and sharks. Five months later, Vanderbilt was gone as well, dying of heart failure in January 1944. Touching tributes poured in for the popular yachtsman, and "few failed to

Alva Base, Fisher Island. *Suffolk County Vanderbilt Museum.*

recognize," Consuelo recalled, "that there was something fundamentally so good and kind in him."[182]

With Harold S. "Mike" Vanderbilt, Willie's younger brother by six years, brought a sea change in personalities. A serious and determined young man who moved through life with quiet purpose, Mike completed both Harvard and Harvard Law and had a mind akin to a frictionless logic machine. He was the originator of contract bridge, determining risks and developing strategy in card playing that would also be skills useful in yacht racing. While bound from Newport to New York aboard his motor yacht *Vara*, one of Mike's friends, asked where they were. "What time is it?" the ever-calculating Vanderbilt replied, sitting in a cabin with his back to the sea, and then added, "Well, let's see":

> *We left the tennis club at 6:18 and left the Ida Lewis Yacht Club at 6:25. It would take us about four minutes to get to* Vara, *and we took five minutes for a swim. That would make it 6:34. It takes two minutes to get the anchor up and get away…6:36. We would be off Fort Adams at 6:40 and off Brenton Reef at 6:50. Point Judith would be about 7:20 and, allowing for the tide, we would be off Watch Hill at 8:21. It was 8:33 when I asked the time. I think if you look out this port beside me, you will see the Fisher's Island Club.*[183]

Mike joined Willie at the New York Central Railroad after law school, where their father was president, and would still be involved decades later when control of the line was lost in a proxy battle in 1954. Neither Vanderbilt brother, however, pursued their business interests with the intensity of their forebears, and it was the allure of sailing that captivated Mike at an early age. He was skippering his own fourteen-foot sloop at twelve and by eighteen was at the helm of *Trivia*, a Herreshoff twenty-five-footer. Big boat experience began with his seventy-six-foot schooner, *Vagrant*, which was built for him by Herreshoff while he was still at Harvard Law. In 1910, he won the Bermuda Race on corrected time with his new yacht. In subsequent years, there would be a second and larger *Vagrant*, the eighty-foot Starling Burges–designed M-class *Prestige* and Olin Stephens–designed twelve-meter *Vim*, which were all actively campaigned. By the end of his racing career, Mike had won a remarkable eight Astor and seven Kings Cups, which were among yachting's most coveted trophies.

His thrice defense of the America's Cup in the 1930s, along with that of Charlie Barr at the turn of the twentieth century, remain unparalleled in the history of that competition. So much has been written about these matches that we need not revisit them here. It suffices to say that, at the helm of the huge J-class sloops *Enterprise* (1930), *Rainbow* (1934) and the super 135-foot J *Ranger* (1937), he was victorious. Olin Stephens, who sailed with Vanderbilt, noted in his autobiography, while he would not have listed him "with the world's greatest helmsmen,"[184] it was Vanderbilt's intelligence,

Ranger crossing the finish line to win the third race of the 1937 America's Cup off Newport. *Author's collection.*

determination and experience, "aided by a clear view of his purpose," that made him a winner.[185] Vanderbilt would also own a number of tenders and cruisers built at Bristol by the Herreshoffs. *Magistrate*, launched in 1916, was just 63 feet, 3 inches overall but had the look of the famous yard's early flyers. Used as the tender for *Vagrant*, it does not appear to have had much in the way of accommodations but was an example of her owner's preference for practicality. With his involvement in the America's Cup came *Vara*, the 150-foot motor yacht launched in 1929, which would be his floating home during the 1930s. Celluloid images of the diesel-powered yacht portray it towing cup defenders off Newport or being equally at home anchored in the East River abreast of the New York Yacht Club's station for commuters during the business week. While built by the Herreshoff Manufacturing Company, the famous yard had been acquired by the Haffenreffer family in 1924, and for *Vara*'s design, Mike had turned to the Purdy Boat Company of Port Washington, New York.

Ned and Gil Purdy were at the peak of their careers in the 1920s and '30s with a client list that included Walter P. Chrysler, Nelson Doubleday and Jock Whitney. Their elegant commuters and sleek Gold Cup racers were the cat's meow, and it's clear Vanderbilt got a state-of-the-art motor yacht. *Vara*, however, would be one of Purdy's largest commissions and had a near sister ship with several sheets of shared plans with *Shadow K*, another 150-foot cruiser, which was built four years earlier for Carl Fisher. Noteworthy features included an outboard rudder and a pair of big Treiber 750-horsepower diesels that moved it along smartly. The bachelor's amenities included a smoking room on the bridge deck, while the main deckhouse comprised two staterooms with full baths and a dining room with fireplace. Olin Stephens remembered that Vanderbilt's afterguard, who lived aboard during the America's Cup summer of '37, had a certain routine. The day commenced with his brother, Rod, and Mike working out on deck before breakfast. Following a day of sailing, dinner would be aboard *Vara*, along with bridge in the evening. Thinking both the stakes and protracted concentration required were beyond his reach, he "was careful to admit no knowledge of the game" although he played at home.[186]

Vara would serve Vanderbilt for a few more seasons, as he had *Prestige* in commission in 1938, winning his sixth King's Cup, and he campaigned his new twelve-motor *Vim* thereafter. However, with the increasing likelihood of the nation's involvement in the war in Europe, Vanderbilt sold his $750,000 motor yacht to the Navy in the fall of 1940 for $125,000.

Mike Vanderbilt's 150-foot *Vara*, built by Herreshoff and designed by Purdy Boat Company, would serve as tender for a number of his racing yachts. Here it tows his America's Cup defender *Rainbow* back to Newport during the 1934 match against T.O.M. Sopwith's *Endeavour. Author's collection.*

During World War II, the USS *Valiant* was engaged in escorting convoys in the Gulf of Mexico and Caribbean. It survived the conflict but was not reacquired after the war by Vanderbilt, who would own an Olin Stephens–designed motor-sailer, *Versatile*, and an eighty-eight-foot ketch.

Among the America's Cup defenders, later achievements were his involvement in rewriting yacht racing's rules, serving as president of Vanderbilt University's board during racial integration and reacquiring Marble House, which had passed out of his family's ownership, and presenting it to the Preservation Society of Newport County. Yet half a century after his demise, there is much that remains unanswered about the famous yachtsman. He was not gregarious, could be difficult and had his share of dustups with race committees. Vanderbilt, who had no children and would not marry until he was forty-seven, also had a long relationship with Eleonora Sears. An extraordinary sportswoman from a prominent Boston Brahmin family, "Eleo," as she was known, was a champion tennis player and an accomplished equestrian with a well-

Mike and Gertrude Vanderbilt on their honeymoon at Cannes in 1933. *Author's collection.*

known sexual preference for her own gender. It's noteworthy, however, that his marriage to Gertrude Lewis Conway of Philadelphia took place the year his mother died. The famously domineering Alva was a disruptor of all of her family members' lives. In Gertrude, Mike found a kindred spirit who shared his passion for sailing and came from a family awash in yachting and Newport associations. Her stepfather, W. Barklie Henry, a good sailor in his own right, was a cousin of A.J. Drexel and a member of both the New York and Corinthian Yacht Clubs of Philadelphia. Barklie M. Henry, her stepbrother, married Gertrude Vanderbilt and Harry Payne Whitney's daughter, Barbara. Mike's bride would be aboard his America's Cup defender in '34 and '37 as timekeeper and Gertrude would be with him through his remaining years. They are interred together at St. Mary's Episcopal Church in Portsmouth, Rhode Island.

21

HENRY WALTERS

(1848–1931)

For Henry Walters, privacy may have been the greatest privilege his fortune would ensure. The famously reserved chairman of the Atlantic Coast Line, the railroad that served much of the Southeast, is probably best remembered today as the founder, along with his father, William, of the Baltimore art gallery that bears their name. Newport's summer colony, however, at the turn of the twentieth century, saw a different side. While at the shore, Walters, an avid yachtsman who would serve as vice-commodore of the New York Yacht Club (1903–6), was known for lavish parties aboard his steam yacht *Narada* and his unconventional domestic arrangements.

On moving to Wilmington, North Carolina, in 1889 to become general manager of the Atlantic Coast Line, Walters contracted typhoid and was nursed to recovery in the home of Pembroke "Pem" and Sarah "Sadie" Jones. The young couple were leading figures in Wilmington, where Pem had a rice milling business and had served as commodore of the venerable Carolina Yacht Club. With shared interests in yachting and art, they became inseparable friends, and in the 1890s, business caused Walters to spend much of the year in New York. The Joneses followed. The threesome were soon residing together, whether in the Joneses' residences in Manhattan and Newport or aboard Walters's 225-foot *Narada*, leading some sly observers to call Sadie the "woman with two husbands."

While there were voyages to Europe with the Joneses to acquire art, *Narada*'s real role was as a stage for Sadie's legendary entertaining, a passion kindled early in life when acting as the Washington hostess for her father, a

Narada, Henry Walters's 225-foot, brigantine-rigged, steam yacht, was the venue for some of Sadie Jones's legendary parties. *The Mariners' Museum and Park, Narada 36851.*

Henry Walters (*front seat, far right*), Sadie (*back seat, far left*) and Pembroke Jones (*second from left behind driver*). *Public domain.*

North Carolina congressman. The myriad press accounts of the Hungarian band playing for lunches, tea dances and dinners aboard the *Narada* while at Newport were beyond comparison. For a luncheon for the Duchess of Marlborough, the salon and tables were bedecked with American Beauty roses, while at a dinner for Prince Cantacuzène and his American fiancée, ices were served in the imperial colors of Russia against a background of intertwined American and Russian flags. Egypt was the theme on another occasion, with lotus flower centerpieces and an Egyptian palmist. But nothing eclipsed a dinner held during *Narada*'s first season at Newport. The thirty-six who boarded on an August evening were seated at a table on deck at the center of which was a ten-foot floral model of the yacht on a lake bordered by aquatic foliage and night-blooming water lilies, which also appeared in the guests' finger bowls. High atop the floral display, even the yacht's burgee, private signal and ensign were depicted in bloom.

Henry Walters owned *Narada* for thirty-four years, during which time it was often moored in Newport. Built in 1889 by Ramage and Ferguson, the well-regarded Scottish yard, Walters acquired the 225-foot brigantine-rigged

Seen here to the right of the Lime Rock Lighthouse (later the Ida Lewis Yacht Club) is *Narada*, which was a familiar sight in Newport during the thirty-four years it was owned by Walters. *Author's collection.*

steam yacht a decade later from A.J. "Tony" Drexel, the son of the famous Philadelphia financier.

Ashore after renting for a number of seasons, the Joneses bought Friedheim, Theodore A. Havemeyer's Bellevue Avenue residence. The sugar baron's ungainly Victorian cottage would soon be improved by the talented New York architect Frances L.V. Hoppin, a well-known member of the summer colony, whose client list included novelist Edith Wharton. Sherwood, as the Joneses renamed the place, would be Newport's version of the White House, and Sadie, outliving both the men in her life, summered there for many years.

Socially ambitious, the Joneses consulted Harry Lehr, the Gilded Age arbiter and confidant of Mrs. William Astor, on how to enter New York society. Southern cooking and hospitality paved the way, as the North Carolinians, with their large African American staff from Wilmington, quickly won over Gotham's elite. Their "table groaned under the weight of rare Southern delicacies," Elizabeth Drexel Lehr recalled, and in the era before cocktails, "No one in Newport could produce mint juleps to equal those Mrs. Pembroke Jones dispensed."[187] Pem joined the New York Yacht Club, winning a number of races with his sloop *Carolina* and was soon called, around Newport, the "commodore of the Thirty Footer Fleet." Pem died in 1919, however, and Henry Walters, in the interest of appearances, moved from the residence at 5 East 61st Street in Manhattan, which the threesome had been sharing, to a nearby hotel. Three years later, on April 11, 1922, from their cabin aboard the Cunard liner *Aquitania*, as it prepared to get underway for Europe, Sadie and Henry announced they had been married that afternoon in a private ceremony and sailed off into the night and into eternal speculation about Newport's ménage à trois.

22

HARRY PAYNE WHITNEY

(1872–1930)

Harry Payne Whitney married Gertrude Vanderbilt in 1896, the year the young couple acquired The Reefs, a mid-nineteenth-century Italianate villa on Bellevue Avenue, which they had the tastemaker Ogden Codman improve. Whitney Cottage, as it would then be known, and where Gertrude, the art patron and sculptress, built a Shingle-style studio, was close to unassuming in comparison to the vast pile her parents completed in Newport the year before, The Breakers.

In marrying the boy next door—their Fifth Avenue mansions in Manhattan were not far apart—Gertrude had not only forged a union between two of the nation's wealthiest families but also brought into the realm of the summer colony a young man who would become one of the Gilded Age's greatest sportsmen. A ten-goal polo player, Harry was one of the "Big Four," the first American team to wrest from the British, in 1909, the International Polo, or Newport Cup, as it is sometimes referred to, having first been played for there in 1876. Whitney also foxhunted with the Meadow Brook Hunt, was interested in coaching and horse shows and inherited from his father in 1904 one of the country's leading racing stables. By the mid-1920s, Harry had more than two hundred Thoroughbreds and was the leading breeder of his era, establishing a phenomenal Triple Crown record, winning two Kentucky Derby races, six Preaknesses and four Belmont Stakes.

How he had time for other interests is remarkable, but Whitney was also a member of six yacht clubs and had a slew of sail and steam yachts.[188] He and good friend H.B. Duryea owned *Yankee*, one of the Newport Seventies,

Harry (*second from left*) was part of polo's "Big Four," the first American team to wrest the International Polo, or Newport Cup, as it was also known, from the British. *Author's collection.*

the 106-foot sloops built by Herreshoff, in which they competed against Gertrude's brother Cornelius, cousin Willie K. Vanderbilt and August Belmont Jr. He also owned the New York Yacht Club Fifty *Barbara*, one of the one-design class sloops introduced in 1913 that were 72 feet overall, and in the late 1920s acquired *Vanatie*, the America's Cup defense candidate, after it had been re-rigged as a staysail schooner. Just how often he was at the helm of his racing yachts, and particularly in his later years, is a question. The able Bostonian Robert W. Emmons, America's Cup skipper Charles Francis Adams and George Nichols frequently stood in for the great equestrian. However, that was not always the case.

The *Philadelphia Enquirer* reported on July 3, 1921, that *Vanatie* had arrived in Marblehead from Newport to join the New York Yacht Club cruise and "would be sailed tomorrow by her owner, Harry Payne Whitney, owing to the slight illness of her skipper, Robert W. Emmons" and that "Mr. Whitney sailed the fifty footer, *Barbara*, some years ago with considerable success."[189]

Steam yachts were also a family tradition. Harry's uncle Colonel Oliver H. Payne, the Ohio industrialist, owned one of the largest such vessels ever built in the United States. Launched in 1898 at the Bath Iron Works in Maine, *Aphrodite* was a 302.6-foot steel-hulled, bark-rigged world traveler on which his bachelor uncle took many long voyages before turning it over to the Navy

Whileaway, Whitney's 177-foot, posh and surprisingly fast houseboat. *Author's collection.*

at the outset of World War I. Colonel Payne's unhappiness, however, with his brother-in-law William C. Whitney's infatuation with a young widow, whom he married after the death of Harry's mother, Flora Payne Whitney, led to a great rift, dividing the family. Harry's brother, William Payne Whitney, sided with his uncle and dropped his first name. Payne Whitney, as he would then be known, inherited part of his uncle's estate after his death in 1917 and the *Aphrodite*. After it was returned by the government in 1919, Payne kept the huge yacht in commission until his own untimely death while playing tennis at age fifty in 1927, but Harry, with an inheritance from his father, would have his own steam yacht.[190]

Whileaway, the 177-foot oil-fired steam yacht Harry commissioned in 1915, was a radical departure from *Aphrodite* and the vessels being built by his peers for round-the-world voyages. Designed by Cox & Stevens and built by Willam Cramp & Son shipbuilding company in Philadelphia, it reflected its owner's interest in coastal cruising and exploring inland waterways. Plate-glass windows replaced portholes on the upper decks, and with a generous beam of 24 feet, *Whileaway* was often classed as a houseboat. However, drawing just 7 feet, 4 inches and with two Parsons turbines pushing it along at a brisk 21 miles per hour, this was something of a deception, as *Whileaway* doubled as a versatile express cruiser, perfect for running back and forth to New York, viewing Harvard-Yale boat races and America's Cup trials. It was also Harry's means of accessing the high-goal polo matches at

Narraganset Pier, where some of the nation's top teams competed on four fields maintained by the Point Judith Country Club, with stabling nearby for one thousand ponies. On one such occasion in August 1916, the Whitneys brought a large party over from Newport to see Great Neck take on Meadow Brook. However, *Whileaway*'s place in history would come the next summer when Whitney, an avid Yalie, put the yacht at the service of the First Yale Unit, an undergraduate flying club organized by his friend H.P. Davison's son, Trubee, then training in flying boats on Long Island's North Shore. Dubbed "The Millionaire's Unit" by the press, the small band of collegians turned naval reservists would distinguish itself in combat after America entered World War I and played an important part in the development of naval air power.

P.A.B. WIDENER

(1834–1915)

For the Wideners, the dawn of the twentieth century brought the best of times and the worst of times. Nothing seemed to be beyond the reach of Peter A.B. Widener, the son of a brickmaker who had started out as a butcher's boy apprentice. Adept at business, he parlayed profits from an initial investment in a chain of butcher shops into a sprawling public transit system empire. This remarkable Philadelphia financier would then help organize U.S. Steel and American Tobacco and was also a significant shareholder in Standard Oil and the parent company of the White Star Line, which owned the *Titanic*. A white star was emblazoned on the Widener's private signal flag flying from the family's yacht.

An art collector on an epic scale, Widener's collection included works by Rembrandt, Rubens, Raphael, Turner, Manet, Renoir and a host of other major artists. Completed in 1900, to the designs of Philadelphia's Horace Trumbauer, Lynnewood Hall in Elkins Park, Pennsylvania, P.A.B.'s immense country seat, housed comfortably both his art treasures and family in its 110 rooms. His sons, George D. Widener, who married Eleanor Elkins, the daughter of his father's business partner, and Joseph E. Widener, and their wives and children all resided at Lynnewood. The family that lived together also played together and shared an interest in yachting and its capital, Newport.

In 1896, the year P.A.B.'s steam yacht *Josephine*, named for his wife, was launched, he joined the New York Yacht Club and his sons soon followed. George's five-year-old daughter, Eleanor, broke the bottle of champagne

Left: P.A.B. Widener. *Author's collection*.

Below: *Josephine* (II), the Wideners' 257-foot steam yacht registered in both P.A.B. Widener and his sons' names, was well known in Newport, where the family leased cottages for the season. *Detroit Publishing Company Collection, Library of Congress*.

Bound for Newport at night and unaware of naval maneuvers that were underway, *Josephine* was fired on by the big guns at Fort Greble on Dutch Island. *National Archives.*

against the bow of the 225-foot steel-hulled vessel, festooned with code flags and the nation's colors, as it slid down the ways. Amenities included a desalinization plant, ice-making equipment and a fireplace and piano in the mahogany-paneled saloon. The Wideners' enjoyment of the yacht would be brief, however; with the outbreak of the Spanish-American War two years later, the *Josephine* was acquired by the Navy.

As the USS *Vixen* (PY.4), it distinguished itself at the Battle of Santiago and during one mission in Cuban waters with Colonel Theodore Roosevelt aboard. The Navy held onto *Vixen* after the war, and the yacht saw service during World War I.

Widener moved quickly to replace the *Josephine* with a larger and more powerful yacht. At 257 feet overall, the $500,000 *Josephine* (II) could move along at eighteen knots with its huge quadruple expansion steam engines and had a larger cruising radius thanks to added coal bunker capacity. Captain S.G. Chase, commander of the previous *Josephine*, was in charge of the new yacht, whose construction he had supervised with Widener.

Press accounts from this century's first decade indicate *Josephine* (II), which would be registered in the names of both father and sons, was a familiar sight at Newport, where various Wideners also leased cottages for the season, including, at various times, Beaulieu, Stoneacre and Pinard. The yacht's arrival in August 1903 must have been particularly memorable for those aboard. Steaming in at night, *Josephine* (II) was unaware of naval maneuvers then in progress. Searchlights at Fort Greble on Dutch Island, near the entrance to Narragansett Bay, detected the yacht underway. The sentries, mistaking it for a ship in the Atlantic Fleet's attacking squadron, sounded general quarters and Fort Greble's big guns opened fire as searchlights at Fort Wetherill at the tip of Conanicut Island and Fort Adams at Newport soon also played on the *Josephine* (II). Luckily for the yacht, the rounds used for the exercise were blanks, and it reached the anchorage unscathed, except for the nerves of those on board and the cacophony.[191]

Eleanor Widener and the rest of the women who boarded the *Titanic's* lifeboats thought their husbands would be following in other boats. *The Miriam and Ira D. Wallach Division of Art, Prints and Photographs: Print Collection. The New York Public Library. "Mrs. George Widener."*

Returning from several months abroad in the spring of 1912, George D. Widener; his wife, Eleanor; and their son Harry Elkins Widener boarded the *Titanic* for its maiden voyage. The Wideners dined with Captain Edward Smith on the night of April 14, when the great liner, driving through ice fields at twenty-three knots, struck the iceberg at 11:40 p.m. Eleanor Widener later recalled the "shock was not very severe."[192] They went on deck and put on their life preservers but "had not the slightest thought that the *Titanic* would sink and only went into the boats at the insistence of our husbands, expecting they would follow in other lifeboats."[193] As her boat pulled away, she saw her husband and son waving and, during the long night that followed, took turns at the oars, relieving exhausted sailors.

Devastated in the aftermath, Eleanor was unaccepting of the loss of her husband and son. Soldiering on, she attended a memorial service in Philadelphia a week after the tragedy. Notably absent was P.A.B. Widener, who was said to be too despondent to attend.

Eleanor recovered in time and went on, in 1915, to complete Miramar, the Bellevue Avenue cottage in the image of a Louis XVI chateau she had planned with George. Dressed in black tulle and wearing the $250,000 string of pearls that had been given to her by her husband, she welcomed the summer colony to a housewarming that would not be soon forgotten. "Supper was served in a room especially erected on the north terrace and enclosed in painted canvas" as the guests danced to the music of three orchestras in the ballroom and on the terraces by the sea.[194]

Horace Trumbauer, who owed a great deal of his career to the patronage of the Elkins and Wideners, was the architect of Miramar and would also design Harvard University's Harry Elkins Widener Memorial Library, a fitting tribute to Eleanor's son, who was a bibliophile and popular member of the college's class of 1907. At the dedication of the library, Eleanor met Harvard professor and explorer Dr. Alexander Hamilton Rice Jr., whom she married thereafter and with whom she would spend a great deal of time at Miramar in the years to come.

P.A.B. Widener never recovered from the loss of his son and grandson. His health failed, and at the time of his death at Lynnewood Hall in 1915, his physicians acknowledged that the *Titanic* disaster had been a contributing cause.

The horrific tragedy would also claim the yacht. Declaring he would never set foot aboard the *Josephine* (II) again, the scene of so many enjoyable cruises with his son, Widener left the yacht laid up on the Delaware River. In the spring of 1916, six months after his death, it was sold to the Russian government and sailed for Archangel. As the armed yacht *Gorislava*, it would change hands a number of times during World War I. Seized by the British in 1918, it served briefly in the Royal Navy before being returned to the Russians the following year.

NOTES

Introduction

1. Garner Dunton, "Newport's Glamour of 1937 Will Be Missing at America's Cup," *New York Times*, September 14, 1958.
2. Ibid.
3. Ibid.
4. Ibid.
5. Mary Cremmen, "Former Newport Splendor Recalled by Cup Races," *Boston Globe*, September 20, 1958.
6. The Newport Casino was the venue for the national tennis championship from 1881 to 1915. International polo made its debut in 1886 at Newport when Britain's Hurlingham Club trounced James Gordon Bennett Jr.'s Westchester Polo Club. The U.S. Open and Amateur in Golf were first played at the Newport Country Club in 1895.
7. Stephens, *The Seawanhaka Corinthian Yacht Club: Origins and Early History* (New York: Sewanhaka Corinthian Yacht Club), 15
8. "Snow White Sails," *New York Telegram*, July 13, 1882.
9. Pierre (IV) and his younger brothers, George L. and Louis L. Lorillard, were all yachtsmen, and one of the tobacconists' brands was Lorillard's Yacht Club Smoking Tobacco. Pierre owned the schooner *Vesta*, one of the three competitors in the Great Ocean Race of 1866, and the steam yacht *Radha*, named for a Hindu goddess. He famously sold his Newport villa, The Breakers, to Cornelius Vanderbilt II in 1882 as he departed to create the Orange County, New York community that would become known as Tuxedo Park. George, who had sailed on *Vesta* in the

transatlantic race, owned a number of well-known yachts but gave up yachting for the turf at the age of twenty-nine in 1872. Louis, who would inherit Vinland at Ochre Point from his aunt Catherine Lorillard Wolfe, actively raced the schooner *Eva*, which was named for his sister and had been previously owned by George. He would later build the big 122-foot Bob Fish–designed *Wanderer*.

10. Bennett would acquire and improve, in the early 1880s, Stone Villa, the venerable Italianate manor house built by Alexander McGregor, the stonemason for Fort Adams, which, before the Civil War, had been the summer retreat of the Middletons of Charleston. The alterations, including a large addition, were overseen by the Newport architect Dudley Newton and gateposts adorned with owls, Bennett's favorite motif, were added at this time. Symbolizing the wisdom of the *Herald*'s words, owls also arrayed the roofline of the paper's Manhattan headquarters, a magnificent Venetian palazzo designed by McKim, Mead and White, and later graced his yachts, cufflinks and even the corners of his unmarked tombstone in Paris.

11. Julius Chambers, "Mr. Bennett's Death a Great Loss to American Journalism," *Brooklyn Daily Eagle*, May 15, 1918, 1.

12. Ibid.

13. John Rousmaniere, *Seafarers: The Luxury Yachts* (Alexandria, VA: Time-Life Books, 1981), 112.

14. "Winchester Makes Record Run," *Brooklyn Daily Eagle*, August 7, 1911.

15. Named for the heroine of Alfred de Mussett's poem, *Namouna* was designed by St. Clair Byrne, the British naval architect who was later responsible for William K. Vanderbilt's *Alva* and *Valiant*. Later sold to the Colombian navy, she would sail on forever in the expatriate artist Julius LeBlanc Stewart's sensual masterpiece, *The Yacht Namouna In Venetian Waters*.

16. "A Lively Day in Newport," *New York Times*, August 19, 1884.

17. "A Buoy for Mr. Bennett's Yacht," *New York Times*, May 29, 1884. When not on a cruise to Ceylon or some distant port, the great yacht could often be seen moored off his villa at Beaulieu near Monte Carlo. On the eve of the First World War in 1914, he sold the *Lysistrata* to the Imperial Russian Navy for use as a hospital ship. Four years later, the *Pawtucket Times* reported on August 21, 1918, that the famous yacht was now at Archangel and had been stripped by the Bolsheviks to a "mere skeleton." The Soviets, however, would continue to make use of it as a fishery patrol craft until after World War II.

18. *New York Times*, June 16, 1904.

19. "Racing for the Goelet Cup," *New York Herald*, August 7, 1884.

20. *Newport Mercury*, August 12, 1893.

21. "The Goelet Cup Races," *New York Times*, August 6, 1887.

22. "The Goelet Cup," *New York Times*, August 13, 1893.

23. "Yacht Races Again Postponed," *New York Times*, August 7, 1884.

24. "The Revival of Yachting," *Illustrated American*, May 27, 1893.

25. Shelley L. Dowling, *Elbridge Thomas Gerry: An Exceptional Life in Gilded Age Gotham* (Clark, NJ: Talbot Publishing, 2017), 237.

26. John Parkinson Jr. in his history of the New York Yacht Club indicates the cost of acquisition was $12,500, and $2,000 more was required for the construction. See John Parkinson Jr., *The History of the New York Yacht Club* (New York: New York Yacht Club, 1975), 140. In 1894, Robert Goelet purchased, at auction, the other half of the property, giving the yacht club control over the entire head of the wharf (see *New York Times*, July 29, 1894). The lease arrangement at the time Station No. 6 was replaced by a new building, the gift of George F. Baker Jr., noted that "the lease of the Gerry and Goelet estates for fifteen years will soon be signed by the New York Yacht Club for its Newport Station, with an option of its purchase" (see "Plan New Yacht Station," *New York Times*, May 22, 1915). The club would maintain Station No. 6 until the property was sold in 1945.

27. "Live Yachting Questions," *New York Times*, November 29, 1891.

28. "Yachting Is on the Move," *New York Times*, October 13, 1889.

29. Some of the resort's most celebrated villas were built by yachtsmen or their wives, including Beacon Rock, Beacon Hill House, Bonniecrest, the first Breakers, Clarandon Court, The Elms, Harbour Court, Mable House, Ochre Court, Rosecliff, Rough Point, Shamrock Cliff, Sherwood and Whitehall.

30. Nancy Randolph, "N.Y.'s Social Center Is Now 200 Miles Away," *Chicago Tribune*, August 16, 1934.

Chapter 1. William Vincent Astor

31. Alfred M. Caddell, "A Young Millionaire at Work," *Brooklyn Daily Eagle*, October 28, 1928.

32. Justin Kaplan, *When the Astors Owned New York* (New York: Viking Penguin, 2006), 32.

33. William P. Stephens, *Traditions and Memories of American Yachting, the 50th Anniversary Edition* (Brooklin, ME: WoodenBoat Publication, 1989).

34. *Brooklyn Daily Eagle*, August 7, 1879.

35. "Mr. Astor's Nourmahal," *Brooklyn Daily Eagle*, March 30, 1884.

36. "Unlucky Yacht Nourmahal," *New York Times*, October 12, 1893.

37. Ibid.

38. Clinton Crane, *Clinton Crane's Yachting Memories* (New York, D. Van Nostrand Company, 1952), 63.

39. Ibid., 64.

40. Gheradi Davis, *Alice and I Down East* (New York: Privately printed at the Gilles Press, 1922), 13.

41. "Astor Brings Home His $600,000 Yacht," *New York Times*, July 4, 1928.

42. Bill Robinson, *Legendary Yachts* (New York: Macmillan Company, 1971), 101.

43. "At Sea where the President Escapes the Care of State," *United States News*, April 2, 1934.
44. Elliott Roosevelt, ed., *FDR, His Personal Letters* (New York: Duell, Sloan and Pierce, 1950), 394.
45. "Yacht Nourmahal Offered for Sale," *New York Times*, August 4, 1948.
46. "U.S. Changes Plans on Nourmahal Sale," *New York Times*, June 25, 1964.
47. The wreck was salvaged the next year.

Chapter 2. George F. Baker Jr.

48. The west side pier and the other *Viking* stories in this chapter were passed on to the author by George F. Baker Jr.'s grandsons, George F. Baker III and Anthony K. Baker.
49. Bill Robinson, *The World of Yachting* (New York: Random House, 1966), 201.
50. "The Talk of the Town," *The New Yorker*, December 21, 1946, 17.
51. "New Giants of Wall Street—George F. Baker, Jr.," *Brooklyn Daily Eagle*, September 17, 1916.
52. Sherman Hoyt, *Sherman Hoyt's Memoirs* (New York: D. Van Nostrand Company, 1950), 253.
53. Ibid.
54. Clarence Michalis (1921–2018) recollections from his ROTC summer cruises aboard the *Viking* were told to the author. He was also recorded by the New York Yacht Club's oral history program.

Chapter 3. August Belmont Jr.

55. "Augie's" great-uncle War of 1812 hero Commodore Oliver Hazard Perry was also a Rhode Island native.
56. "August Belmont's New Yacht," *New York Times*, January 17, 1900.
57. Christopher Pastore, *Temple to the Wind* (Guilford, CT: Lyons Press, 2005), III.
58. "*Mineola*'s First Sail," *New York Times*, May 8, 1900.
59. David Black, *The King of Fifth Avenue: The Fortune of August Belmont* (New York: Dial Press, 1981), 665.
60. "Young Belmont's Rage," *New York Times*, July 2, 1883.
61. Eleanor Robson Belmont, *The Fabric of Memory* (New York: Farrar, Strauss and Cudahy, 1957), 85.

Chapter 4. John R. Drexel

62. Dan Rottenberg, *The Man Who Made Wall Street* (Philadelphia: University of Pennsylvania Press, 2001), 176.
63. "John R. Drexel, 72, Dies in Paris Home," *New York Times*, May 19, 1935.
64. "Consigned to the Sea," *New York Times*, December 19, 1899.
65. "John R. Drexel, 72, Dies."
66. William F. Rasmussen, "Course of the Steam Yacht Sultana's Owner J.R. Drexel 1890-91-92," unpublished diary, Drexel University Archives, Philadelphia, Pennsylvania.
67. "*Sultana* to Stay in France," *New York Times*, May 2, 1898.
68. *Brooklyn Daily Eagle*, May 8, 1899.
69. Cornelius Vanderbilt Jr., *Queen of the Golden Age*, 2nd ed. (Maidstone, UK: George Mann Books, 1999), 171.
70. Ibid.
71. "Famous Yacht Doomed," *New York Times*, January 6, 1937.

Chapter 5. Julius Forstmann

72. *New York Times*, September 20, 1929, 10.
73. Roger Vaughan, *The Strenuous Life of Henry Anderson* (Mystic, CT: Mystic Seaport, 2013), 2–4.

Chapter 6. Harriette Warren Goelet

74. Captain John Carley (1833–1912), who had gone to sea on a whaler at thirteen and run through Confederate blockades during the Civil War, supervised the construction of the William Townsend–designed *Norseman* at the Polilon yard in Brooklyn in 1881 (see "Captain John Carley Dead," *New York Times*, January 5, 1912).
75. "Women Members of the New York Yacht Club," *New York Sunday World*, September 5, 1901.
76. "Mrs. Goelet Takes Trip in Submarine Octopus," *Brooklyn Daily Eagle*, July 27, 1911.
77. Harriette W. Goelet letter to Robert W. Goelet, February 21, 1908, private collection.
78. "American Boat Victorious," *New York Times*, June 29, 1902.
79. The *Hohenzollern* had brought the kaiser's brother, Prince Henry, over for the launching of the emperor's new racing yacht, the *Meteor III*. For an account of the kaiser's tribute to Beatrice, see "German Kaiser's Tribute," *New York Times*, February 17, 1902.
80. Harriette W. Goelet letter to Robert W. Goelet, February 23, 1900, private collection.
81. Ibid., April 10, 1905.

82. Ibid., March 28, 1903.

83. "Anthony J. Drexel Dies At 70," *New York Times*, December 15, 1934.

84. "Mrs. Goelet Pays Damages," *New York Times*, May 13, 1906.

85. Harriette W. Goelet letter to Robert W. Goelet, April 24, 1903.

86. "Queen of the Rum Fleet Held," *New York Times*, April 27, 1924.

87. "Dry Chief Canfield Visits Rum Fleet off Jersey; Here Are Some of the Vessels He Encountered," *Brooklyn Daily Eagle*, April 20, 1923.

88. Ibid.

89. Malcolm F. Willoughby, *Rum War at Sea* (Washington, D.C.: Treasury Department, 1964), 46.

90. Erik Hofman, *The Steam Yachts: An Era of Elegance* (Tuckahoe, NY: John DeGraff, 1970), 102.

Chapter 7. Huntington Hartford

91. "Ocean Race Start Recalls Old Days," *New York Times*, August 27, 1937.

92. Encountering a gale in the race back to Newport, the *Conrad* lost a mast, allowing *Seven Seas* to win easily.

Chapter 8. Howard Hughes

93. Bruce Sherman, "Hughes Was Here, Remembered, Too," *Newport Mercury*, February 11, 1972.

94. Peter Harry Brown and Pat H. Broeske, *Howard Hughes: The Untold Story* (New York: Penguin Books, 1996), 86.

95. Ibid.

96. "John Jacob Astors Give First Dinner," *New York Times*, July 27, 1934.

97. "British Blacklist a Famous Yacht," *New York Times*, April 12, 1942.

98. "Mrs. Mackay Life One of Adventure," *New York Times*, May 15, 1928.

Chapter 9. Arthur Curtis James

99. "Arthur Curtis James, Railroad Financier, Died," *New York Herald Tribune*, June 5, 1941.

100. Ibid.

101. "Reflections on Arthur Curtiss James 1867–1941: Commodore 1909–1910," by Roger Vaughan, as abridged by Commodore Harry Anderson, unpublished memorandum, New York Yacht Club.

102. Crane, *Clinton Crane's Yachting Memoirs*, 34.

103. Ibid.

104. "The Aloha Launched," *Brooklyn Daily Eagle*, June 22, 1899.

105. Maud Howe Elliot, *This Was My Newport* (Cambridge, MA: Mythology Company, 1944), 211.

106. Robinson, *Legendary Yachts*, 43.

107. "Arthur C. James's Yacht Saluted at Newport As It Sails for the First Time This Season," *New York Times*, May 14, 1928.

108. The Lime Rock Light was renamed Ida Lewis Light in 1924 in honor of the nineteenth-century keeper's daughter, who is said to have saved eighteen lives.

109. "Steamer Collides with *Aloha*; 6 Hurt," *New York Times*, September 28, 1931.

110. "Yacht *Aloha* Strikes Boat off New Haven," *New York Times*, August 9, 1934.

111. "Hartman Again Arrested," *New York Times*, July 23, 1923.

112. "*Aloha* to Be Broken Up," *New York Times*, October 2, 1937.

113. Roger Vaughan quotes extensively from the *Newport Mercury* of October 16, 1937, which included these observations. See Vaughn, *Arthur Curtis James: Unsung Titan of the Gilded Age* (Sonoma, CA: Story Arts Media, 2019, 336.

114. Ibid.

Chapter 10. Sir Thomas J. Lipton

115. "Whole City Turns Out to Greet Lipton and *Shamrock*," *Newport Daily News*, August 22, 1930.

116. Elliot, *This Was My Newport*, 199.

117. "Lipton's *Shamrock V* Arrives for Races," *New York Times*, August 14, 1930.

118. Edith's husband was the chairman of the Lackawanna Steel Company and grandson of one of the founders of New York's National City Bank. Married in Newport in 1896, the Taylors had deep roots among the cottagers. Edith's father-in-law H.A.C. Taylor's iconic Newport residence on Annandale Road, designed by McKim, Mead and White, had helped introduce the Colonial Revival to America and stood next to The Cliffs, her mother-in-law Charlotte Fearing Taylor's family's cottage. Her sister, Harriet, who was married to James F. D. Lanier, spent summers at Gravel Court off Clay Road. *Nieuport*, Edith's thirty-one-foot, six-inch sloop, was designed by the talented naval architect William Gardner and built at City Island, New York, by Henry B. Nevins in 1920. For many years, she could be found moored off the Taylors' boathouse and dock at The Glen, a gentleman's farm at Portsmouth, Rhode Island, on the Sakonnet River where Edith and Moses built their John Russel Pope–designed French chateau.

119. Plant's penchant for whims knew no bounds, and the man who would trade his Manhattan townhouse for a strand of pearls fancied by his second wife, thirty years his junior, was soon on to something else. Following a thirty-three-thousand-mile cruise aboard *Iolanda* in 1909–10, his attention turned to his next endeavor, the great Herreshoff schooner *Elena*, and the steam yacht was sold to a

Russian acquaintance, Elizabeth Terestchenko of St. Petersburg, the widow of a Ukrainian sugar magnate. Her ownership would also prove fleeting.
120. "Lipton Receives Newport's Gifts," *New York Times*, September 21, 1930.

Chapter 11. H. Edward Manville

121. "Young Manville Wed Here," *New York Times*, July 3, 1911.
122. "Mrs. V.C. Manville Dead Here at 74," *New York Times*, August 25, 1941.
123. "Yachting Parties Held at Newport," *New York Times*, September 20, 1934.
124. *Dictionary of American Naval Fighting Ships*, vol. 5 (Washington, D.C.: Navy Department, Office of the Chief of Naval Operations, Naval History Division, 1970), 80.

Chapter 12. Jesse H. Metcalf

125. Frederick B. Gifford, "Presidential Visits," Squantum Association, www.squantumassociation.com; *Newport Mercury*, August 22, 1932.
126. "J.H. Metcalf Dies; Former Senator," *New York Times*, October 10, 1942.
127. "Schooner *Druid* Sunk," *New York Times*, July 27, 1902.
128. "Senator Enjoys Rest on Yacht," *Van Wert Daily Bulletin*, July 5, 1929.
129. "Threatens Inquiry on Liquor Killings," *New York Times*, January 1, 1930.
130. Ibid.
131. "Senator Metcalf for Dry Law Repeal," *New York Times*, October 23, 1930.

Chapter 13. Ogden L. Mills

132. George Plimpton, "The Many Sided Character of Harold Vanderbilt," *Sports Illustrated*, October 1956.
133. "Carnegie Charters Yacht," *New York Times*, June 19, 1916.
134. "Lends Steam Yacht as Ambulance Ship," *New York Times*, May 28, 1917.
135. "Crew of Rum Yacht Get Light Penalty," *New York Times*, December 17, 1931. The yacht and cargo were forfeited to the government by consent of the owner, Arthur Deery of Manhattan, in exchange for light sentences for the crew.

Chapter 14. E.D. Morgan

136. Stephens, *Traditions and Memories of American Yachting*, 232.
137. *New York News*, July 10, 1892.
138. A.J. Kenealy, "Yachting," *Outing*, August 1891.

139. Sherman Hoyt, *Sherman Hoyt's Memoirs* (New York: Van Nostrand Company, 1950), 6–7.
140. "The *Catarina* Mishap," *New York Times*, October 26, 1890.
141. Edwin Denison Morgan, *Recollections for My Family* (New York: Charles Scribner & Son, 1938), 98–99.
142. "A Yacht for the Shamrock," *New York Times*, August 15, 1898.
143. "News of Newport," *New York Times*, September 9, 1912.

Chapter 15. J.P. "Jack" Morgan

144. "Floating Palace for Thomas W. Lawson," *New York Times*, April 28, 1900.
145. "Morgan Yacht Hits Maine Rock: Breaking Up of New $2,500,000 Corsair Feared with 11-Foot Drop of Penobscot Bay Tide," *New York Times*, September 3, 1930.
146. Accompanying their grandfather were Jack and Henry Morgan, George Nichols Jr. and Paul Pennoyer. The story is told in Robert M. Pennoyer's wonderful memoir *As It Was* (Westport, CT: Prospecta Press, 2015).

Chapter 16. Frederick H. Prince

147. Crane, *Clinton Crane's Yachting Memoirs*, 186.
148. *Brooklyn Daily Eagle*, September 16, 1938.
149. Don McLennan, "A Line on Liners," *Brooklyn Daily* Eagle, August 15, 1935.
150. Prince was also a member of the New York Yacht Club and many other clubs.
151. Palmer H. Fletcher, MD, "An Association with Frederick H. Prince III and F.H.P. Jr. Summers of 1932, 1933, 1934 and 1935," private collection.
152. Carlyle Hoyt, "Prince Tax Hearing Sheds Light on Millionaire's Life," *Boston Globe*, November 30, 1939.
153. "Masts of America's Cup Yachts to Be Higher Than Enterprises," *New York Times*, January 14, 1934.
154. "Diesel Yacht Dodges Waterspouts on Maiden Trip," *Brooklyn Daily Eagle*, July 14, 1929.
155. Happily, the torpedo was not armed but would have done serious damage had it struck one of the yachts (see "Torpedo Nearly Hits Astor Yacht," *Brooklyn Daily Eagle*, August 13, 1937).

Chapter 17. T.O.M. Sopwith

156. Alan Bramson, *Pure Luck* (Wellingborough, UK: Patrick Stephens Limited, 1990), 143.
157. Ibid.

158. Ibid.
159. "New Fokker Yacht Slides into Grief," *New York Times*, June 21, 1938.
160. Ibid.

Chapter 18. Cornelius "Neily" Vanderbilt

161. "Yachting Parties Held at Newport," *New York Times*, September 20, 1934.
162. Cornelius Vanderbilt Jr., *Queen of the Golden Age: The Fabulous Story of Grace Wilson Vanderbilt* (Maidstone, UK: George Mann Books, 1999), 265.
163. Ibid.
164. *Brooklyn Daily Eagle*, August 21, 1900.
165. "To Repair the Winchester," *New York Times*, May 9, 1930.
166. Vanderbilt, *Queen of the Golden Age*, 397.
167. Ibid.

Chapter 19. Frederick W. Vanderbilt

168. Most likely Nelson of Paris who, a few years before, had furnished *Mayflower* and *Nahma* for the Goelet brothers. The Vanderbilt yacht's paneling is described in "The Warrior," *The Rudder* 15 (January–December, 1904): 531.
169. "Gives Up Yachting," *Pawtucket Times*, May 20, 1914.
170. Gertrude Vanderbilt Whitney.
171. "Vanderbilt Yacht in Dock," *New York Times*, August 14, 1924.

Chapter 20. William K. Vanderbilt II and Harold S. "Mike" Vanderbilt

172. Kenneth T. Jackson, *Crabgrass Frontier: The Suburbanization of the United States* (New York: Oxford University Press, 1985), 99.
173. Consuelo Vanderbilt Balsam, *The Glitter and the Gold* (New York: St. Martin's Press, 1953), 13.
174. "New London to Newport," *New York Herald*, August 9, 1889.
175. "'Arrest Me Every Day If You Want To' Says Mr. Vanderbilt," copyright 1900 by W.R. Hearst as quoted by Steven H. Gittelman, *Willie K Vanderbilt II: A Biography* (Jefferson, NC: McFarland & Company, 2010), 39.
176. "Vanderbilt Tells Why He Quits Newport," *Newport Journal*, September 16, 1901.
177. Balsam, *Glitter and the Gold*, 8.
178. "The News of Newport," *New York Times*, April 17, 1899.

179. Seawanhaka had sponsored the nation's first open amateur regatta off Newport in 1872.

180. Crane, *Clinton Crane's Yachting Memoirs*, 80.

181. Ibid., 8.

182. Balsam, *Glitter and the Gold*, 235.

183. Russell Owen, "Harold S. Vanderbilt Races His Yachts and Plays Bridge With a Single Eye For Victory…and Usually Gets It," *New York Times*, August 18, 1940.

184. Olin J. Stephens, *All This and Sailing Too* (Mystic, CT: Mystic Seaport, 1999), 90.

185. Ibid.

186. Ibid., 111.

Chapter 21. Henry Walters

187. Elizabeth Drexel Lehr, *King Lehr and the Gilded Age* (Philadelphia: J.B. Lippincott Company, 1935), 67.

Chapter 22. Harry Payne Whitney

188. New York, Larchmont, Manhasset Bay, Montauk, Newport and Royal Thame Yacht Clubs.

189. *Philadelphia Inquirer*, July 3, 1921.

190. *Aphrodite* was part of the Breton Patrol during World War I, the small fleet of American yachts engaged in convoy off the French coast.

Chapter 23. P.A.B. Widener

191. "Blank Shots Fired at Yachts," *New York Times*, August 24, 1903.

192. "George D. Widener," *New York Tribune*, April 21, 1912.

193. Ibid.

194. "Mrs. G.D. Widener Opens New Villa," *New York Times*, August 21, 1915.

SELECTED BIBLIOGRAPHY

Allen, Armin Brand, *The Cornelius Vanderbilts of The Breakers: A Family Retrospective*, 2nd ed. Newport, RI: Preservation Society of Newport County, 2005.

Balsam, Consuelo Vanderbilt. *The Glitter and the Gold*. New York: St. Martin's Press, 1953.

Belmont, Eleanor Robson. *The Fabric of Memory*. New York: Farrar, Strauss and Cudahy, 1957.

Bramson, Alan. *Pure Luck*. Wellingborough, UK: Patrick Stephens Limited, 1990.

Brewster, Hugh. *Gilded Lives, Fatal Voyage*. New York: Crown Publishing, 2012.

Brown, Peter Harry, and Pat H. Broske. *Howard Hughes: The Untold Story*. New York: Penguin Books, 1996.

Carosso, Vincent P. *The Morgans: Private International Bankers 1854–1913*. Cambridge, MA: Harvard University Press, 1987.

Crane, Clinton. *Clinton Crane's Yachting Memories*. New York: D. Van Nostrand Company, 1952.

D'Antonio, Michael. *A Full Cup: Sir Thomas Lipton's Extraordinary Life and His Quest for the America's Cup*. New York: Riverhead Books, 2010.

Davis, Deborah. *Gilded: How Newport Became America's Richest Resort*. Hoboken, NJ: John Wiley & Sons Inc., 2009.

Davis, Gheradi. *Alice and I Down East*. New York: Privately printed at the Gilles Press, 1922.

Dinn, Alan E. *Boats by Purdy*. St. Michaels, MD: Tiller Publishing, 2003.

Downing, Antoinette F., and Vincent J. Scully Jr. *The Architectural Heritage of Newport, Rhode Island, 1640–1915*. 2nd ed. New York: Bramhall House, 1967.

Elliot, Maud Howe. *This Was My Newport*. Cambridge, MA: Mythology Company, 1944.

Friedman, B.H. *Gertrude Vanderbilt Whitney*. Garden City, NY: Doubleday & Company Inc., 1978.

Gubernick, Lisa Rebecca. *Squandered Fortune: The Life and Times of Huntington Hartford*. New York: G.P. Putnam's Sons, 1991.

Haviland, William A., and Barbara L. Britton. *Floating Palaces: America's Queens of the Seas*. Stonington, ME: Penobscot Books, 2016.

Hofman, Erik. *The Steam Yachts: An Era of Elegance*. Tuckahoe, NY: John DeGraff Inc., 1970.

Holm, Ed. *Yachting's Golden Age 1880–1905*. New York: Alfred A. Knopf, 1999.

Hoyt, Sherman. *Sherman Hoyt's Memoirs*. New York: D. Van Nostrand Inc., 1950.

Jackson, Kenneth T. *Crabgrass Frontier: The Suburbanization of the United States*. New York: Oxford University Press, 1985.

Jobson, Gary. *An America's Cup Treasury: The Lost Levick Photographs*. Newport News, VA: Mariners' Museum, 1999.

Johnston, William R. *William and Henry Walters, The Reticent Collectors*. Baltimore: Johns Hopkins University Press, 1999.

Kaplan, Justin. *When the Astors Owned New York*. New York: Viking Penguin, 2006.

Katherens, Michael C. *Newport Villas: The Revival Styles, 1885–1935*. New York: W.W. Norton & Company Inc., 2009.

Knight, Lucia del Sol, and Daniel Bruce MacNaughton. *The Encyclopedia of Yacht Designers*. New York: W.W. Norton & Company, 2006.

Lehr, Elizabeth Drexel. *King Lehr and the Gilded Age*. Philadelphia: J.B. Lippincott Company, 1935.

Logan, Sheridan A. *George F. Baker and His Bank 1840–1955*. n.p., privately printed, 1981.

MacKay, Robert B. *Great Yachts of Long Island's North Shore*. Charleston, SC: Arcadia Publishing, 2014.

MacKay, Robert B., Anthony K. Baker and Carol Traynor, eds. *Long Island Country Houses and Their Architects, 1860–1940*. New York: W.W. Norton & Company Inc., 1999.

MacTaggart, Ross. *The Golden Century: Classic Motor Yachts 1830–1930*. New York: W.W. Norton & Company, 2001.

McKee, Fraser. *The Armed Yachts of Canada*. Erin, ON: Boston Mills Press, 1983.

Miller, Paul F. *Lost Newport: Vanished Cottages of the Resort Era*. Carlisle, MA: Applewood Books Inc., 2009.

Moore, C. Philip. *Yachts in a Hurry: An Illustrated History of the Great Commuter Yachts*. New York: W.W. Norton & Company, 1994.

Morgan, Edwin Denison. *Recollections for My Family*. New York: Charles Scribner & Sons, 1938.

Newport Reading Room Sesquicentennial History. Newport, RI: Privately printed, 2003.

The New York Yacht Club: A History, 1844–2008. New York: New York Yacht Club, 2009.

Paine, Ralph D. *The Corsair in the War Zone.* Boston: Houghton Mifflin Company, 1920.

Parkinson, John, Jr. *The History of the New York Yacht Club.* New York: New York Yacht Club, 1975.

Pastore, Christopher. *Temple in the Wind*, Guilford, CT: Lyons Press, 2005.

Pennoyer, Robert M. *As It Was.* Westport, CT: Prospecta Press, 2015.

Rasmussen, William F. "Course of the Steam Yacht Sultana's Owner J.R. Drexel 1890-91-92." Unpublished diary, Drexel University Archives, Philadelphia, Pennsylvania.

Robinson, Bill. *Legendary Yachts.* New York: MacMillan Company, 1971.

———. *The World of Yachting*, New York: Random House, 1966.

Roosevelt, Elliott, ed. *FDR, His Personal Letters.* New York: Duell, Sloan and Pierce, 1930.

Rose, H. Wickliffe. *Brittany Patrol.* New York: W.W. Norton & Company, 1937.

Rottenberg, Dan. *The Man Who Made Wall Street.* Philadelphia: University of Pennsylvania Press, 2001.

Rousmaniere, John. *The Golden Pastime: A New History of Yachting.* New York: W.W. Norton & Company, 1986.

———. *The Luxury Yachts.* Alexandria, VA: Time-Life Books, 1981.

Schroder, Walter K. *Dutch Island and Fort Greble.* Charleston, SC: Arcadia Publishing, 1998.

Stensrud, Rockwell. *Newport: A Lively Experiment 1639–1969.* Newport, RI: Redwood Library and Athenaeum, 2015.

Stephens, Olin J. *All This and Sailing Too.* Mystic, CT: Mystic Seaport, 1999.

Stephens, W.P. *The Seawanhaka Corinthian Yacht Club: Origins and Early History.* New York: Seawanhaka Corinthian Yacht Club, 1963.

———. *Traditions and Memories of American Yachting, the 50th Anniversary Edition.* Brooklin, ME: WoodenBoat Publications, 1989.

Strouse, Jean. *Morgan: American Financier.* New York: Random House, 1999.

Vanderbilt, Cornelius, Jr. *Queen of the Golden Age: The Fabulous Story of Grace Wilson Vanderbilt.* Maidstone, UK: George Mann Books, 1999.

Vaughan, Roger. *Arthur Curtiss James: Unsung Titan of the Gilded Age.* Sonoma, CA: Story Arts Media, 2019.

———. *The Strenuous Life of Harry Anderson.* Mystic, CT: Mystic Seaport, 2013.

Wilson, Derek. *The Astors: 1763–1992.* New York: St. Martin's Press, 1993.

Yarnall, James L. *Newport Through Its Architecture.* Newport, RI: Salve Regina Press, 2005.

ABOUT THE AUTHOR

Robert B. MacKay is a lifelong sailor and classic boat enthusiast who received his doctorate in American and New England Studies from Boston University in 1980. He dates his interest in yachting history to having been a member of Rudy Schaefer's crew that sailed his replica of the schooner yacht *America* from Newport to England in 1968. Among his recent books are *America by the Yard: Cirkut Camera Images from the Early Twentieth Century* (W.W. Norton, 2006), *Great Yachts of Long Island's North Shore* (Arcadia Publishing, 2014) and *Marine Paintings at the New York Yacht Club* (2019). He also wrote the introduction to Phil Moore's *Yachts in a Hurry* and was editor of *Long Island Country Houses and Their Architects, 1860–1940*. He is Director Emeritus of Preservation Long Island and former chairman of the New York State Board for Historic Preservation.